THE
Breadmaker Bible

THE
Breadmaker Bible

Crostini to Croutons, Sourdough to Stollen
New ideas, clever techniques and exciting recipes

Karen Saunders

EBURY PRESS
LONDON

For Sonia and Simon

First published in Great Britain in 2003

1 3 5 7 9 10 8 6 4 2

First published by Ebury Press,
Random House, 20 Vauxhall Bridge Road, London SW1V 2SA

Random House Australia (Pty) Limited
20 Alfred Street, Milsons Point, Sydney, New South Wales 2061, Australia

Random House New Zealand Limited
18 Poland Road, Glenfield, Auckland 10, New Zealand

Random House South Africa (Pty) Limited
Enulini, 5A Jubilee Road, Parktown 2193, South Africa

The Random House Group Limited Reg. No. 954009

www.randomhouse.co.uk

A CIP catalogue record for this book is available from the British Library

ISBN 0 091 88925 1

Editor Amanda Howard
Project Manager Claire Wedderburn-Maxwell
Designers Grade Design Consultants, London
Photographer Craig Robertson
Home Economist Karen Saunders
Food Stylist Angela Boggiano
Stylist Helen Trent

Colour separation by Icon Reproduction
Printed and bound in Singapore by Tien Wah Press

Contents

Introduction

What is it about breadmakers? I remember my first conversation with Sonia Allison and discussing this very point. Little did we know then just where that conversation would lead us.

Both of us could hold our own where food, cooking and baking were concerned and both of us had started dabbling with these curious, new, trendy kitchen gadgets. In the beginning they seemed almost alien to us as we'd both learned to bake the traditional way, but destiny was taking us down the same path: my job – advising consumers and writing bread recipes for Allinson flour – meant I had had to become a dab hand at using breadmakers in a very short space of time; and, recognising the potential of this market, Sonia had started sowing the seeds for what was to become her *Complete Bread Machine Cookbook*.

Between us we spent endless days trying out different recipe combinations, Sonia in Watford and me in Wiltshire, our experiences enlivened by many lengthy telephone conversations comparing notes. And we had wonderful afternoons together laughing about our trials and tribulations while enjoying one of Sonia's fabulous home-made cakes.

Sonia's sudden death in the summer of 2002 put an untimely end to our union. Our friendship gave me great joy and I am reminded of Sonia's determination and spirit every time I bake a loaf. It is an honour and a pleasure to continue her work and further our collective cause with the production of this book.

Starting to use a breadmaker throws up a host of immediate questions and challenges. What is this plastic cup for? Which yeast and flour should I use? Why must I add the ingredients in a certain order, and what's the difference between the white, wholemeal and French programmes? When Sonia first started her book there was a need for clear, concise explanation; consumers wanted a recipe book that was allied to British baking and one that bridged the gap between cup measures and good old grams and ounces. *The Complete Bread Machine Cookbook* did this perfectly and so, in writing its sequel, I have moved on a stage. In this book you will still find all the basic information you need if you're a complete novice, but also recipes tempting enough to guide you to more advanced baking. But central to the philosophy of this book is making your daily bread work for you.

So, whether you're looking to find loaves to complement special dietary requirements, to boost nutrients for children, or the best bread for barbecues, breakfasts and packed lunches, it's all here in one essential volume. I've also enlisted the help of my good friend Dan De Gustibus, the award-winning artisan baker and proprietor of the De Gustibus bakeries and cafés in London. I've had the pleasure of working with Dan on many projects over the years and we've mixed a good few doughs together. I thank him for his inspiration for the wonderful breadmaker sourdoughs in this book.

Karen Saunders

The Breadmaker Phenomenon

I'd class myself as a bit of a cook, the sort of person you'd expect to have a breadmaker. But breadmakers attract more than just us cooks. They've become less scary than a hand-mixer and trendier than espresso machines and everyone seems to have one. Just think, how many times have you heard 'Oh, and I got a breadmaker for Christmas'? I mean, my father, who incidentally is the sort that eats baked beans from the tin, and my sister, the queen of convenience food, have both readily turned their hands to breadmaking using these marvellous machines. And both of them regularly produce an impressive repertoire that makes the bread fixtures of your average supermarket look decidedly dull.

Making bread in a breadmaker is a whole new experience. If you're a seasoned bread machine owner you'll realise, as Sonia and I did, that everything you may once have learned about yeast cookery is mostly irrelevant. Using a breadmaker needs an entirely different approach – maybe that's why my dad and my sister can do it so well and why Sonia and I had to start from scratch.

Getting to know your breadmaker is very important. Tedious as it may seem, it's important to know how the cycles work, how the dough should look and feel at every stage and also how the machine sounds. Can you tell if your machine is kneading a stiff or a soft dough by the sound it makes? Well, if you make a habit of listening and lifting the lid to feel the dough as it's worked you'll learn the characteristics of the best dough for your particular model. By doing this you'll be able to make adjustments to recipes during the kneading cycles should your dough be too wet or too dry. This means you can put any potential problems right before it's too late.

Helpful Hints

Successfully using a breadmaker is easy as long as you follow a few basic rules:

• If you are new to baking with a breadmaker, take the time to read the hints and tips in this book and in your manufacturer's handbook before you start. Then practice with basic loaves until you are familiar with how your machine works before moving on to the more advanced recipes.

• Measure your ingredients carefully and accurately. Either use the plastic cup provided with your machine or metric or imperial measures. Follow one set of measures only; NEVER mix them. ALWAYS use the plastic spoon provided for measuring teaspoons and tablespoons. NEVER use household cutlery as their size varies greatly.

If you're a fan of grams and ounces, I strongly recommend investing in a set of electronic scales that measure both liquid (ml/fl oz) and dry ingredients (g/oz) for the best results. In most cases you can stand the breadmaker bucket on top of the scales and measure directly into it, which is much quicker and it saves washing up.

Date and Walnut Bread

• Always use instant or fast-acting dried yeast (also called easy-bake yeast). This yeast is available in sachets and now in larger packs that are more convenient if you bake every day. Be particular about the storage and use-by information on the packet and don't try and save partially used sachets for next time – the yeast will become inactive and your bread will not rise.

Do not use fresh yeast in your breadmaker. Although some manufacturers persist in recommending traditional dried active yeast (usually sold in tins), I would not advise it for breadmaker use. This yeast is designed for traditional hand baking and is best used only for this purpose.

• Always add the ingredients in the order specified for your particular model. Most machines put the wet ingredients in first, followed by the flour and then the yeast. Some machines advise the reverse – adding the yeast first, then the dry ingredients followed by the liquid. If your machine recommends this, then, when using my recipes, simply reverse the order in which the ingredients are added to the bucket by reading the list from bottom to top. In both cases the aim is to keep the yeast away from the moisture; as soon as yeast meets moisture it starts to activate and you don't want this to happen until your bread starts mixing to ensure there is enough power left in the yeast to rise the bread.

Some books also recommend keeping the sugar and salt away from the yeast. If you get into the habit of adding liquid, sugar, salt, flour then yeast – or completely reversing this order – then you'll soon find you do this automatically. Sonia's method was to add half the flour, then the sugar and salt and then the other half. I always forgot to do this, so all my recipes follow the sequence I've outlined, with the exception of the sourdough-style recipes where I've kept the salt and sugar away from the delicate starter by using the flour as a buffer.

• Although some instruction books advise against lifting the lid, I'd definitely advise you to look at your dough as it's mixing and kneading. It's even worth having a quick feel of it. Also, listen to the motor of your machine and, with practice, you'll find you are able to judge whether it's kneading a stiff dough or mixing a soft one just by the sound of it. This will all help build your knowledge of what a good dough looks and feels like; and, as you become more experienced, you'll know whether the dough is just right, too wet or too dry. Do not lift the lid during the rising or baking cycles. The only time I ever do this is to quickly brush on an Egg Wash (see page 163).

• Even though breadmakers control the environment in which they bake the bread, the external environment can still affect them. When in Australia recently I was talking to a bread machine owner about this and she was describing how on really hot and humid days she sometimes cannot produce a satisfactory loaf. It's worth bearing this in mind if you suddenly have a failure of a tried and trusted recipe. Have you just put the central heating on; or is it very hot or humid?

In general keep your machine in a dry and draught-free place at a comfortable room temperature. Never keep it outside or in the garage and never in direct sunlight or next to the hob or oven. Ensure there is ample space around and above your machine for air to circulate and that the air vents are not obstructed. Take care when the machine is baking as the outside can get quite hot and the air vents may puff out steam.

• If you are using a fan oven to bake doughs made in your breadmaker, you may need to reduce the temperature slightly from that given in the recipe – usually by about 10–20°C, depending on the recipe.

• Never put your breadmaker baking pan in the dishwasher as it will damage the paddle mechanism and never use metal utensils in it as they will scratch the non-stick surface. If your paddle gets stuck in the bottom of your bread, carefully remove it with a pair of plastic kitchen tongs, taking care not to damage the non-stick surface of the paddle. It's worth noting that most manufacturers sell extra paddles and buckets, if yours ever need replacing.

• In some recipes it may be necessary to scrape excess flour into the mix/dough from the sides of the bucket as the dough is mixing. This is especially true when making gluten-free or yeast-free bread as the dough is not so elastic and more cake-like. I use a small but long-handled plastic spatula for this purpose (intended for scraping the last bit of sauce from the tomato ketchup bottle!) and it works a treat.

• As there are now so many different breadmakers on the market, with new models coming out all the time, it is impossible within the limits of one book to write recipes for the capacity of every machine. All machines have a cycle based on approximately 450 g/16 oz/3 cups of flour and I have used this as a basis for all the recipes in this book. Recipes for larger loaves based on 600 g/21 oz/4 cups of flour are given in the Basic Breads chapter to help get you started. You can then use these as a guide to gross up quantities for machines with larger capacities.

• As bread machines become more complex their functions include specific cycles for an ever-wider range of bread. For convenience, I have used programmes that are universal to the majority of machines on the market. There's nothing to stop you experimenting with the other programmes; simply follow your manufacturer's handbook and adjust the recipe if necessary.

A lot of the latest machines now have specific cycles for gluten-free loaves. I have found these to be very good for the gluten-free recipes in this book. If you are following a gluten-free diet then buying a machine with this option would be best.

• Although many machines offer jam-making programmes I have not included jam recipes in this book.

• Finally, remember that even though you are using an automatic breadmaker every loaf will be different. That's part of the charm of home baking. The crust colour and texture will vary, as will its smoothness and shape. If you are having particular difficulties, see the Common Problems on pages 165–7. Otherwise, be prepared for variety and enjoy the individual character of your home-made bread.

Store Cupboard Essentials and Breadmaking Ingredients

Fundamentally, bread is a combination of flour, yeast and water. Salt and a sweetener (usually sugar or honey) is added to assist the action of the yeast and the rest is really up to you. There are literally thousands of ingredients that can be added to flavour breads and to vary the texture – the possibilities are truly endless. But before we get carried away with creativity it is essential to understand how each breadmaking ingredient contributes to the final loaf. So take a few minutes to read on – your breadmaking will benefit.

The secret of success is simple. Use the right ingredients, use them correctly and measure them accurately. Once you've mastered this, there will be no looking back.

Wheat Flours

The most common grain used in breadmaking is wheat. The wheat kernel comprises three parts; the bran, the germ and the endosperm. The bran is the husk that encloses the kernel; the nutritious wheatgerm is the seed that would grow into a new plant; and the endosperm is the inner part of the kernel that contains starch and protein. It is the level of protein found in the endosperm that determines whether a flour is ideal for breadmaking. As dough made from high-protein, hard-wheat flour is kneaded, the protein develops into gluten, the elastic substance which forms the mesh-like structure that encapsulates the carbon dioxide bubbles given off by the fermenting yeast. It is the gluten structure that allows dough to develop into the light and airy texture of fresh cooked bread.

As breadmaking has become more popular, the choice of bread flours on the market has grown. Alongside strong white and wholemeal flour you'll find other interesting varieties like brown flour with malted flakes and white flour with grains of rye and wheat. By making your own bread you can decide on a unique combination of flours to give exactly the

taste and texture you want. Be guided by the recipes in the Basic Breads chapter (see pages 20–43) and experiment with your own flour combinations.

Wheat Bread Flours Used in this Book

STRONG WHITE BREAD FLOUR

The classic white bread flour that, during milling, has the bran and germ removed giving a flour of approximately 70–75 per cent extraction.

VERY STRONG WHITE BREAD FLOUR

This new white bread flour is specially blended from the finest hard wheat varieties, normally from Canada and North America, to give a flour super-high in gluten. I've used this flour widely in this book and it's especially good for breadmakers, giving improved rise and texture to bread, particularly when blended with strong wholemeal flour or flours naturally low in gluten.

STRONG WHOLEMEAL FLOUR

To be called wholemeal this flour must be of 100 per cent extraction. This means that the whole grain is used in its production, including the germ and bran. Therefore the full nutritional value of the grain is retained, making this flour a useful source of B vitamins, calcium, iron and fibre. However, the presence of bran reduces the effectiveness of gluten during baking and hence bread made with only wholemeal flour will not rise as high and will be much denser than its white equivalent. The presence of bran also means that the flour will absorb more liquid, so more water is needed in the dough. When using wholemeal flour in a breadmaker, use only 50 per cent of the total mix: a 50:50 blend with strong white flour or very strong white flour will produce a better texture and a lighter loaf.

STRONG BROWN FLOUR
Brown flour is different to wholemeal in that it is of 90 per cent extraction, i.e. 10 per cent of the bran is omitted. Brown flour is high in nutrients and will still absorb slightly more liquid than white flour. However, it will produce a noticeably lighter loaf than wholemeal, hence it is possible to make excellent 100 per cent brown loaves in a breadmaker.

COUNTRY GRAIN STRONG BROWN BREAD FLOUR
A base of strong brown flour enhanced with malted wheat flakes. This flour is also known as malted wheatgrain or granary.

SOFT GRAIN STRONG WHITE BREAD FLOUR
Strong white flour with added fibre thanks to the addition of cracked wheat and rye grains, which also give bread an interesting texture and additional 'bite'.

Other Flours Used in this Book

It's not just wheat-based flours that can be used for breadmaking. For thousands of years a vast range of dried grains, roots and seeds have been used in bread. These flours tend to have little or no gluten and cannot therefore be used alone to make bread in a breadmaker. They can, however, be blended with strong flours to vary the taste and texture of bread. For coeliac diets, gluten-free flours can be used in a breadmaker but special ingredients need to be added for good results (see page 19).

Below are details of the other flours I have used in the recipes for this book. They can be purchased from health food shops, delicatessens or specialist websites (see suppliers details on page 171).

BARLEY FLOUR
Barley has been used for centuries as a base for bread; in fact, together with oats, it was the usual choice for early bakestone breads here in the UK. Barley flour is low in gluten, grey-brown in colour and gives an earthy tang to bread.

BUCKWHEAT FLOUR
Buckwheat is naturally gluten-free as it is not really a cereal at all. It is native to Russia and is produced from the esculentum shrub, which belongs to the same plant group as rhubarb and the common dock.

The flour, ground from esculentum's triangular seeds that look similar to beechnuts, can be found in good health food shops. Buckwheat flour is grey-brown in colour and has a distinctive, slightly bitter taste.

CORNMEAL (OR MAIZE MEAL)

An excellent gluten-free ingredient for adding both flavour and texture to bread, particularly to gluten-free loaves. It is made from maize – the familiar corn-on-the-cob – and is widely used in American and Italian cooking. From the same origins, but not quite as fine as cornmeal, is polenta, which is also used to give a gritty texture, rich colour and sweet, corn flavour to recipes in this book.

GLUTEN-FREE FLOUR AND GLUTEN-FREE BREAD FLOUR

Generally gluten-free flour is a pre-blended mix of rice, potato, buckwheat, maize, tapioca and other gluten-free flours. It will need to be used with xanthum gum (see page 19) for loaves made in a breadmaker. Also on the market is gluten-free bread flour, again a blend of gluten-free flours but with the xanthum gum already added.

Unlike wheat bread, gluten-free breads are made from a mix that resembles a very thick batter rather than a dough. Because of the lack of elasticity in the mix it will be necessary to scrape down the edges of the bucket with a plastic spatula during the mixing cycle to ensure all the ingredients are incorporated into the batter prior to baking.

Gluten-free loaves will have a different texture to traditional wheat breads and will not rise as high. When baking gluten-free loaves expect a moist, firm, cake-like texture.

GRAM FLOUR

Gram flour or *besun* is made from ground chickpeas and is most commonly used in Indian and Pakistani dishes. Chickpea flour is gluten-free and gives a rich flavour and golden colour to bread even if only added in small quantities.

KUMAT FLOUR

Kumat is closely related to wheat but does not form as strong a gluten structure as wheat. It therefore needs to be mixed with wheat flour for best results, giving its golden yellow colour and excellent flavour to the finished loaf.

MILLET FLOUR

Millet flour gives a lovely natural sweet flavour to bread and, while it's low in gluten, it's a good source of protein, vitamins and minerals.

OATMEAL

Oats have been used for centuries in breadmaking, either as a coarse meal or finely ground into flour. There are many grades: the cleaned hulled grains, called grouts; grouts that have been cut into two or three pieces, called pinhead oats; those that have been ground, oatmeal; and the finest grade, flour. Although oats contain small amounts of gluten some people with coeliac disease can tolerate small quantities of oats, but do check with your doctor or dietitian before introducing them into your diet. Oatmeal is rich in nutrients but relatively high in fat, hence it is an excellent choice for adding extra flavour to breads.

POTATO FLOUR

No prizes for guessing where this one comes from! Potatoes are cooked, dried and then ground to give this brilliant white flour. Historically potatoes were used in Britain as a cheap filler for bread, making the dough go further and providing a favourable ingredient to aid fermentation. Potato still appears frequently in bread recipes today, either raw, mashed or in the form of flour to add moistness to the finished loaf. Note that potato starch is different to potato flour.

QUINOA FLOUR

Translated from the language of the Inca Indians, quinoa means 'mother', a clue to the sacred status it has held for thousands of years. Quinoa was nearly wiped out as the Spanish attempted to obliterate native cultures in the New World, but some strains survived in the remote high plains of the Andes.

Botanically, quinoa is a member of the goosefoot family and is related to spinach, beet and chard. If ever there was an outstanding nutritional food quinoa is it. It contains more protein than a grain and four times as much calcium as wheat. What's more, the protein in quinoa is of better quality than that of meat and it's also rich in iron and vitamins B and E. Quinoa is low in fat, with the majority of its oil being polyunsaturated, providing many essential fatty acids.

Today this valuable crop has enjoyed a resurgence and quinoa is now grown in the high regions of California, Colorado and western Canada.

Quinoa is available as a grain, as flakes and as flour. It has a bitter flavour but its nutritional value makes it a great ingredient for special diets and so where it's used I've either masked it's flavour with other ingredients or added small quantities of flour so it remains unnoticed. Quinoa can be found in health food shops and from specialist websites (see page 171).

RICE FLOUR

Rice flour (not to be confused with ground rice, which is much coarser) is one of the most easy to find non-wheat, gluten-free flours and is available in brown and white varieties. It also forms the base for many of the gluten-free flour blends found on supermarket shelves today. Brown rice flour is made from the whole grain and white rice flour made once the bran and germ have been removed.

White rice flour is a good choice for those following a low-fibre diet.

RYE FLOUR

Rye flour provides the distinctive flavour of many German, Central European and Scandinavian breads. While rye is naturally low in gluten, it will also inhibit the gluten development of high gluten flours it is mixed with so care should be taken when including rye in flour blends. I love rye flour so don't be put off. It provides a rich and distinctive tangy flavour and, when used in moderation, adds a whole new dimension to even the most basic breads. In many of my recipes I add just a few tablespoonfuls and use it like a kind of seasoning. This way you get wonderfully tasty bread and an excellent texture.

SEMOLINA

Semolina is made from durum wheat, the same grain commonly used to make pasta and couscous. It comes from the heart or endosperm of the wheat grain and when added to bread it gives both colour and texture.

SOYA FLOUR

Soya flour is made from soy beans and is an excellent ingredient for enriching bread dough. It is yellow in colour, rich in protein and gluten-free.

SPELT FLOUR

Spelt is a grain closely related to wheat that can be tolerated by some people on wheat-free diets. In addition, there is evidence that the type of gluten found in spelt flour can be tolerated by those with intolerance to wheat gluten. However, if you are sensitive to wheat or gluten it is advisable to consult your GP or dietician before trying spelt bread. Spelt flour makes lovely, light golden bread though I've found it needs more yeast than common wheat flour.

TAPIOCA FLOUR

This brilliant white flour is a useful ingredient for gluten-free breads, strengthening the structure and improving the texture of the finished loaf.

Notes on Storage

FLOUR

Flour should be stored in a cool, dry place – ideally in an airtight container. Pay careful attention to the use-by dates on packaging and always roll down the top of the bag after use. If you only bake occasionally, flour is best stored in the freezer; just ensure that it has time to reach room temperature before attempting to make bread with it.

As wholemeal flour contains more fat than white, it does not keep as long as white flour.

DOUGH

If time is short, bread dough can be frozen for use later as long as it doesn't contain any perishable ingredients or ingredients that are unsuitable for freezing. Seal unshaped dough in an oiled plastic bag, leaving just enough space for the dough to rise slightly as it freezes. It will keep for up to five days. To thaw, place the dough in the fridge for 12–24 hours, until it doubles in size. Remove from the fridge and shape, prove and bake as normal.

BREAD

Only store bread after it has thoroughly cooled. According to your preference, store bread in a clean dry cloth, a sealed plastic bag, or a bread bin at room temperature. Do not store bread in the fridge as this will dehydrate the bread and speed up the staling process.

Cooled baked bread can be frozen either wrapped in foil or a plastic freezer bag. Be sure to push all the air out of the bag before freezing. Bread can be frozen for up to 3 months, but ideally not longer than 3–4 weeks. For best results defrost bread slowly in a cool place or in the fridge for 8–10 hours, then store as above.

Other Ingredients

YEAST

Yeast is a living organism and should always be treated as such. Like us it requires food and warmth to thrive and like us it will die if it gets too cold.

Without resorting to a schoolbook lecture, yeast is needed to turn bread from a solid mass of dough into an air-filled spongy mass that, once baked, will be a delight to eat. How does this happen? By fermentation. During fermentation yeast is activated by liquid and feeds on sugar and the starch from the flour. As it grows, the yeast gives off carbon dioxide and alcohol. When this happens in bread dough the gas bubbles get caught in the mesh-like gluten structure and rise, until finally the heat of the oven kills off the yeast and the starch in the flour sets, holding the shape of the risen loaf.

When baking traditionally you can judge when the optimum fermentation has been achieved and then bake the dough, but in a breadmaker the time of the cycles is strictly regulated, which means that the action of the yeast must be controlled by careful measuring of the ingredients and the use of salt.

In a breadmaker, instant or fast-acting dried yeast makes things a whole lot simpler (see Helpful Hints, page 10) and this is why I'd recommend that you use only this type of yeast in your machine. Instant yeast (also called easy-bake or easy-blend) is simply a combination of dried yeast and, in most cases, vitamin C (ascorbic acid). This yeast is made by removing the moisture from fresh yeast (making it inactive) and drying it. The yeast is compressed into strands that are then chopped to give very fine particles that do not need to go through the rehydration process before being added to the dough mixture. The presence of vitamin C, a natural dough improver, guarantees the fast action of the yeast and works to improve the protein structure, helping the dough to trap carbon dioxide and rise more effectively.

Bear in mind again that yeast is a living organism. The yeast will die if the liquid is too hot or cold. Most breadmakers will gently heat the dough as it mixes so don't worry too much about accurately measuring the temperature with a thermometer to the last degree; simply ensure your ingredients are at room temperature.

Do not use fresh yeast in your breadmaker or traditional dried active yeast (sold in tins) – these are both more suited to baking by traditional methods.

SALT

Salt serves to control the action of the yeast throughout the baking process, gives a well-rounded flavour to the bread and improves the keeping qualities of the loaf. Salt should be used with care as adding too much will kill the yeast and too little will mean that the dough could rise out of control.

I'm often asked about leaving salt out of bread but in my experience, especially in a breadmaker, dough tends to over-rise, giving a poor-quality loaf and a collapsed crust. If you're trying to cut down on salt in your diet remember that compared to processed foods home-made bread is very low in salt. I have used the minimum amount of salt in my recipes wherever possible, and you can always reduce the salt content in the foods you serve with your bread.

SUGAR

Most breadmaker recipes use sugar to give the yeast a quick supply of food to ensure sufficient fermentation occurs within the limits of the machine's cycle. For good measure I always add sugar, honey or other sweet ingredients to my dough. It is possible to use the natural sugars in fruit juice and fruit juice concentrates as an alternative and I have shown you how to use these in the low-sugar recipes in this book.

Be aware that too much sugar will kill yeast. Particular care should be taken with recipes that use more than one sweet ingredient, e.g. syrup, chocolate, fruit, jam or chutney, as the total sugar content could collectively destroy the yeast.

LIQUID

Most commonly water is added to bread dough to give the yeast the moisture it needs to grow; but any liquid can be used to vary the taste and texture of the bread. Milk gives a finer, tender crumb; buttermilk or natural yoghurt a tangy taste; and beer, cold tea, juices and even champagne can be used to add moisture and flavour to the bread.

FAT

In our low-fat culture it's often forgotten that butter or oil is added to bread to enhance it's crumb structure, taste and keeping qualities. Butter, margarine and vegetable oils can be substituted like for like to vary the flavour to suit your taste, but don't use low-fat spreads unless they are designed for baking. Flavoured oils are especially useful for giving additional taste and olive oil adds a wonderful continental touch. For special diets, wherever possible I've used oils high in polyunsaturates or canola oil, which is cholesterol-free.

EGGS

Eggs are great ingredients for enriching bread dough. Always use the correct size of egg stated in the recipe and ensure they are at room temperature before use. If you cannot use fresh eggs for any reason, you can substitute with an egg replacer (available from health food shops) following the instructions on the pack.

FRUIT, NUTS, CHEESE, HERBS AND SPICES

Use common sense when adding these ingredients. Herbs, spices, seeds and cheese can be added with the other dry ingredients. For softer and more fragile ingredients, such as dried or ready-to-eat fruit and nuts, add during the second kneading cycle to retain their shape and to prevent them getting mashed up by the paddle during mixing. Most machines have a 'bleep' to signal when extra ingredients should be added and some models have a little trap door in the lid that automatically drops the ingredients in at the best time. As you become more experienced you will learn how best to add extra ingredients to suit your machine and your taste.

XANTHUM GUM

This is an expensive yet essential ingredient for gluten-free loaves made in a breadmaker. It can be purchased from larger supermarkets, health food shops and specialist websites (see page 171). Like live yoghurt and the friendly bacteria drinks now on the market, xanthum gum is made from a bacterium

and works wonderfully to give improved rise, texture and mouth-feel to gluten-free bread and cakes. Note that xanthum gum does not mix well with water, so always mix it thoroughly with the flour before adding to the breadmaker bucket.

Some gluten-free bread flours already have xanthum gum added, which will save you purchasing it separately, but you will need it if you make your own gluten-free flour blends. Use the recipes in this book to see how xanthum gum should be used and read the label for guidance on quantities when adding it to other gluten-free bread recipes.

Basic Breads

CLASSIC WHITE BREAD

With its light, open texture and golden crust, this versatile loaf is perfect for sandwiches and toast.

225 ml/8 fl oz/1 cup (350 ml/12 fl oz/1½ cups) water

2 tbsp (3 tbsp) melted butter, cooled

1½ tbsp (2 tbsp) sugar

1½ tsp (2 tsp) salt

450 g/16 oz/3 cups (600 g/21 oz/4 cups) strong white bread flour

1¼ tsp (2 tsp) instant or fast-acting dried yeast

glaze/topping (optional, see pages 162–3)

Pour the water into the breadmaker bucket, followed by the butter, sugar and salt. Cover with the flour and finally sprinkle the yeast over. Fit the bucket into the breadmaker and set to the basic white programme for the appropriate size loaf. Once cooked, carefully shake the loaf from the bucket and stand the right way up on a wire cooling rack. Brush with your chosen glaze and add any topping, if using. Leave the bread to cool for at least an hour before cutting and/or removing the paddle if necessary.

SOFT GRAIN BREAD

A white loaf with extra 'bite' from the cracked grains added to soft grain flour. This is a versatile bread that will be loved by all the family.

Follow the recipe for the Classic White Bread (above), replacing the strong white bread flour with soft grain strong white bread flour with kibbled (cracked) grains of rye and wheat.

Soft Grain Bread

LIGHT WHOLEMEAL BREAD

This is the perfect wholemeal loaf for a breadmaker – rich in flavour and lighter in texture than 100 per cent wholemeal bread, which I have never found to be acceptable when made in a bread machine.

225 ml/8 fl oz/1 cup (350 ml/12 fl oz/1½ cups) water

3 tbsp (4 tbsp) sunflower oil

2 tbsp (3 tbsp) runny honey

225 g/8 oz/1½ cups (300 g/11 oz/2 cups) strong wholemeal bread flour

1½ tsp (2 tsp) salt

225 g/8 oz/1½ cups (300 g/11 oz/2 cups) very strong white bread flour

1½ tsp (2½ tsp) instant or fast-acting dried yeast

glaze/topping (optional, see pages 162–3)

Pour the water into the breadmaker bucket, followed by the oil and honey. Cover the liquid with the wholemeal flour and sprinkle the salt over. Add the white flour and top with the yeast. Fit the bucket into the breadmaker and set to the basic rapid/wholemeal rapid or wholewheat programme for the appropriate size loaf. Once cooked, carefully shake the loaf from the bucket and stand the right way up on a wire cooling rack. Brush with your chosen glaze and add any topping (if using). Leave the bread to cool for at least an hour before cutting and/or removing the paddle if necessary.

LIGHT RYE BREAD

This loaf has a close yet light texture, with all the flavour of rye. Try serving it with cold meats and pickles for a taste of the continent.

Follow the recipe for Light Wholemeal Bread (above), replacing the wholemeal flour with rye flour.

COUNTRY BROWN BREAD

A delicious loaf with the distinctive, nutty flavour of brown bread, this bread cuts like a dream.

225 ml/8 fl oz/1 cup (350 ml/12 fl oz/1½ cups) water

2 tbsp (3 tbsp) sunflower oil

2 tbsp (3 tbsp) runny honey

1¼ tsp (1½ tsp) salt

450 g/16 oz/3 cups (600 g/21 oz/4 cups) strong brown bread flour

1¼ tsp (2 tsp) instant or fast-acting dried yeast

glaze/topping (optional, see pages 162–3)

Pour the water into the breadmaker bucket, followed by the oil and honey. Cover the liquid with the salt and flour and finally sprinkle the yeast over. Fit the bucket into the breadmaker and set to the basic white programme for the appropriate size loaf. Once cooked, carefully shake the loaf from the bucket and stand the right way up on a wire cooling rack. Brush with your chosen glaze and add any topping (if using). Leave the bread to cool for at least an hour before cutting and/or removing the paddle if necessary.

RUSTIC RYE BREAD

This loaf has all the texture of a rustic brown bread with the added richness of rye.

250 ml/9 fl oz/1⅛ cups water

2 tbsp sunflower oil

1 tbsp runny honey

1½ tsp salt

150 g/5¼ oz/1 cup country grain strong brown bread flour

150 g/5¼ oz/1 cup rye flour

150 g/5¼ oz/1 cup very strong white bread flour

1½ tsp instant or fast-acting dried yeast

glaze/topping (optional, see pages 162–3)

Pour the water into the breadmaker bucket, followed by the oil, honey and salt. Cover the liquid with the flours and finally sprinkle the yeast over. Fit the bucket into the breadmaker and set to the wholemeal rapid programme. Once cooked, carefully shake the loaf from the bucket and stand the right way up on a wire cooling rack. Brush with your chosen glaze and add any topping (if using). Leave the loaf for at least an hour before cutting and/or removing the paddle if necessary.

MALTED BROWN BREAD

This rustic loaf has all the taste of brown bread and added texture provided by the malted wheat flakes in the flour. It's perfect served sliced or in chunks with everything from soup to cheese.

300 ml/11 fl oz/1³/₈ cups (350 ml/12 fl oz/ 1¹/₂ cups) water

2 tbsp (3 tbsp) sunflower oil

¹/₂ tbsp (1 tbsp) runny honey

1¹/₂ tsp (2 tsp) salt

450 g/16 oz/3 cups (600 g/21 oz/4 cups) country grain strong brown bread flour

1¹/₂ tsp (2¹/₂ tsp) instant or fast-acting dried yeast

glaze/topping (optional, see pages 162–3)

Pour the water into the breadmaker bucket, followed by the oil, honey and salt. Cover the wet ingredients with the flour and finally sprinkle the yeast over. Fit the bucket into the breadmaker and set to the wholewheat/wholemeal programme for the appropriate size loaf. Once cooked, carefully shake the loaf from the bucket and stand the right way up on a wire cooling rack. Brush with your chosen glaze and add any topping (if using). Leave the bread to cool for at least an hour before cutting and/or removing the paddle if necessary.

LIGHTER MALTED BROWN BREAD

A lighter, airy loaf but still with enough malted brown flour to give that distinctive flavour and bite.

Follow the recipe for Malted Brown Bread (above), but use half country grain strong brown bread flour and half strong white bread flour.

Malted Brown Bread

FARMHOUSE LOAF

This bread has the rustic taste and appearance of a traditional farmhouse loaf. Its texture is enhanced with malted wheat flakes and kibbled grains of rye and wheat, with the brown and wholemeal flours contributing to its rich, nutty taste. It's the perfect bread for cheese and chutney sandwiches and it also makes fantastic toast.

225 ml/8 fl oz/1 cup (375 ml/13 fl oz/1⁵/₈ cups) water

3 tbsp (4 tbsp) sunflower oil

2 tbsp (2¹/₂ tbsp) runny honey

2 tsp (2¹/₂ tsp) salt

70 g/2¹/₂ oz/¹/₂ cup (100 g/3¹/₂ oz/³/₄ cup) strong wholemeal bread flour

70 g/2¹/₂ oz/¹/₂ cup (100 g/3¹/₂ oz/³/₄ cup) country grain strong brown bread flour

150 g/5¹/₄ oz/1 cup (190 g/6¹/₂ oz/1¹/₄ cups) soft grain strong white bread flour

150 g/5¹/₄ oz/1 cup (190 g/6¹/₂ oz/1¹/₄ cups) very strong white bread flour

1¹/₂ tsp (2 tsp) instant or fast-acting dried yeast

glaze/topping (optional, see pages 162–3)

Pour the water into the breadmaker bucket, followed by the oil, honey and salt. Cover the liquid with the flours and finally sprinkle the yeast over. Fit the bucket into the breadmaker and set to either the basic white or the wholemeal rapid programme for the appropriate size loaf. Once cooked, carefully shake the loaf from the bucket and stand the right way up on a wire cooling rack. Brush with your chosen glaze and add any topping (if using). Leave the bread to cool for at least an hour before cutting and/or removing the paddle if necessary.

ALL SPELT BREAD

Spelt is a grain that, while closely related to wheat, can be tolerated by some people following a wheat-free diet. It makes a beautiful light brown loaf perfect for all occasions.

225 ml/8 fl oz/1 cup water

1 tbsp sugar

1½ tbsp sunflower oil

¾ tsp salt

450 g/16 oz/3 cups spelt flour

2¼ tsp instant or fast-acting dried yeast

glaze/topping (optional, see pages 162–3)

Pour the water into the breadmaker bucket, followed by the sugar, oil and salt. Cover with the flour and sprinkle the yeast over. Fit the bucket into the breadmaker and set to the basic white programme. Once cooked, carefully shake the loaf from the bucket and stand the right way up on a wire cooling rack. Brush with your chosen glaze and add any topping (if using). Leave the bread to cool for at least an hour before cutting and/or removing the paddle if necessary.

HALF SPELT AND BROWN BREAD

Follow the recipe for All Spelt Bread (above), but use half strong brown bread flour and half spelt flour.

LIGHTER HALF SPELT BREAD

Follow the recipe for All Spelt Bread (above), but use half very strong white bread flour and half spelt flour.

Blended Flour Recipes

There is a huge choice of speciality flours on the market that, while unsuitable for making bread on their own, can be blended with strong bread flour to vary the taste and texture of the finished loaf. Below are some of my favourite variations. It's worth noting when using these flours that the diversity of origins and differences in brands means that there can often be large variations in the flours themselves, which means that their ability to absorb water from the mix can vary from bag to bag. When using these flours, it's best to check the mix during the kneading cycle and add a little more water if necessary.

QUINOA BREAD

Quinoa flour can be found in good health food shops. It is milled from the quinoa grain, though technically quinoa is a fruit. Though still not widely recognised in Britain, quinoa has been grown as a staple food source for over five thousand years. In its native North America, it is known as the 'mother grain' because of its sustaining properties that traditionally have been utilised for those working at high altitudes. As far as nutritional attributes go, quinoa is hard to beat (see page 16 for more information on its dietary value). When blended in small quantities with white bread flour, quinoa gives a golden, rustic-looking loaf with a rich, speckled crust and a soft, open texture – quite delicious.

225 ml/8 fl oz/1 cup water

2 tbsp melted butter, cooled

1½ tbsp sugar

1½ tsp salt

375 g/13 oz/2½ cups strong white bread flour

70 g/2½ oz/½ cup quinoa flour

1¼ tsp instant or fast-acting dried yeast

glaze/topping (optional, see pages 162–3)

Pour the water into the breadmaker bucket, followed by the butter, sugar and salt. Cover with the flours and finally sprinkle the yeast over. Fit the bucket into the machine and set to the basic white programme. Once cooked, carefully shake the loaf from the bucket and stand the right way up on a wire cooling rack. Brush with your chosen glaze and add any topping (if using). Leave the bread to cool for at least an hour before cutting and/or removing the paddle if necessary.

GRAM FLOUR BREAD

Gram or channa dahl is a member of the chickpea family and, not surprisingly, gram flour is a popular ingredient in Eastern cooking. It is a good source of gluten-free protein and, when combined with strong white bread flour, gives a loaf that is beautifully rounded and golden, with a naturally sweet taste and a creamy, moist crumb.

Follow the recipe for Quinoa Bread (see page 31), replacing the quinoa flour with gram flour.

BUCKWHEAT FLOUR BREAD

Buckwheat is gluten-free and a good source of protein and B vitamins. When blended with strong white bread flour the resulting bread is pleasantly speckled and has a warm grey/brown colour. This loaf slices like a dream and has a fine, silky texture suprising from a flour that is not a grain at all but the product of a member of the rhubarb family.

Follow the recipe for Quinoa Bread (see page 31), replacing the quinoa flour with buckwheat flour.

Gram Flour Bread

SOYA FLOUR BREAD

High in protein and complex carbohydrates, soya flour provides both colour and nutrition to bread when combined with strong white bread flour. The loaf has a rich amber crust and a dark golden centre. Its close texture gives a naturally moist loaf that is perfect with both sweet and savoury dishes.

Follow the recipe for Quinoa Bread (see page 31), replacing the quinoa flour with soya flour.

BARLEY FLOUR BREAD

Bread made using barley flour has a well-rounded flavour. It's pleasingly rustic in appearance with a wonderful crust, perfectly complemented by a creamy, light centre.

Follow the recipe for Quinoa Bread (see page 31), replacing the quinoa flour with barley flour.

Soya Flour Bread

RICE FLOUR BREAD

Rice flour gives a smooth, golden and well-risen loaf with a light and silky texture.

Follow the recipe for Quinoa Bread (see page 31), replacing the quinoa flour with rice flour.

KUMAT FLOUR BREAD

Kumat is a grain that is closely related to wheat, though the gluten structure it forms during breadmaking is not as strong as that of common wheat. When mixed with white flour, however, it makes a lovely loaf with a golden-yellow colour and good flavour. An excellent choice if you want to add more variety to your bread.

Follow the recipe for Quinoa Bread (see page 31), replacing the quinoa flour with kumat flour.

MILLET FLOUR BREAD

While millet flour may be low in gluten, it is very rich in protein, vitamins and minerals. It gives a natural sweet flavour to bread and makes a pleasing speckled, golden-crusted loaf.

Follow the recipe for Quinoa Bread (see page 31), replacing the quinoa flour with millet flour.

Millet Flour Bread

French Bread Recipes

We all love French breads, whether they're baguettes, sticks or the traditional freeform loaves now found in most supermarkets. One of my greatest disappointments when I was a new bread machine owner was that the manual included only one standard white French bread recipe. When I saw for myself what this cycle could produce, I immediately got to work developing more recipes for it and now we can create the full range of French breads at home. The breadmaker result might be loaf shaped, but it will still have the promise of a crisp crust and that distinctive light and airy centre. Like all French breads, these loaves are best eaten fresh.

BASIC FRENCH BREAD

The classic French-style loaf with a crisp, golden crust and light, airy centre. As this bread contains no fat it stales quickly, so it's best eaten on the day of baking.

225 ml/8 fl oz/1 cup water

1½ tbsp sugar

1½ tsp salt

450 g/16 oz/3 cups very strong white bread flour

1¼ tsp instant or fast-acting dried yeast

glaze/topping (optional, see pages 162–3)

Pour the water into the breadmaker bucket, followed by the sugar and salt. Cover the liquid with the flour and finally sprinkle the yeast over. Fit the bucket into the breadmaker and set to the French programme. Once cooked, carefully shake the loaf from the bucket and stand the right way up on a wire cooling rack. Brush with your chosen glaze and add any topping (if using). Leave the bread to cool for at least an hour before cutting and/or removing the paddle if necessary.

BROWN FRENCH BREAD

While this loaf will not rise as high or be quite as light as its white counterpart, the added texture of brown flour in a French bread makes this an excellent variation.

Follow the recipe for Basic French Bread (see opposite), increasing the water by 2 tbsp and using half strong brown bread flour and half very strong white bread flour.

FRENCH GARLIC AND HERB BREAD

This light, airy and aromatic loaf is richly flavoured and has a golden crust and speckled centre. It's perfect served as it is with a hearty casserole or enhanced still further by smothering with Garlic and Herb Butter (see page 164).

225 ml/8 fl oz/1 cup water

2 tbsp olive oil

2 tsp sugar

1 tsp salt

1½ tsp minced dried garlic granules

1½ tsp dried herbes de Provence

450 g/16 oz/3 cups strong white bread flour

1¼ tsp instant or fast-acting dried yeast

glaze/topping (optional, see pages 162–3)

Pour the water and olive oil into the breadmaker bucket, followed by the sugar, salt, garlic and herbs. Cover with the flour and sprinkle the yeast over. Fit the bucket into the breadmaker and set to the French programme. Once cooked, carefully shake the loaf from the bucket and stand the right way up on a wire cooling rack. Brush with your chosen glaze and add any topping (if using). Leave the bread to cool for at least an hour before cutting and/or removing the paddle if necessary.

FRENCH ONION BREAD

The addition of dried onion flakes gives a wonderful flavour to the finished bread. I always add them with the flour and let the machine mash them up while kneading as this means that there are no pieces of onion to interfere with the wonderful light, airy texture of this delicious bread. If you'd prefer to maintain the texture provided by the onion flakes, add them during the second kneading cycle – but remember, as most French programmes don't include a bleep for added ingredients, you may need to set a kitchen timer to remind you!

250 ml/9 fl oz/1 1/8 cups water

2 tsp melted butter, cooled

2 tbsp sugar

2 tsp salt

400 g/14 oz/2 3/4 cups very strong white bread flour

25 g/1 oz/5 tbsp dried onion flakes

1 1/4 tsp instant or fast-acting dried yeast

glaze/topping (optional, see pages 162–3)

Pour the water into the breadmaker bucket, followed by the butter, sugar and salt. Cover the liquid with the flour. Finally, put the onion flakes on top of the flour at one side of the bucket and the yeast at the other. Fit the bucket into the breadmaker and set to the French programme. Once cooked, carefully shake the loaf from the bucket and stand the right way up on a wire cooling rack. Brush with your chosen glaze and add any topping (if using). Leave the bread to cool for at least an hour before cutting and/or removing the paddle if necessary.

CHÈVRE FRENCH BREAD

Chèvre means 'goat' in French and this loaf makes the most of the tangy flavour of goats' cheese. A thick, crispy crust surrounds this richly fragrant bread, which makes a tasty accompaniment to vegetable dishes.

225 ml/8 fl oz/1 cup water

2 tbsp olive oil

1 tsp salt

2 tsp sugar

50 g/2 oz/½ cup finely diced goats' cheese

4 tbsp dried chopped chives

400 g/14 oz/2¾ cups strong white bread flour

4½ tbsp rye flour

1 tsp instant or fast-acting dried yeast

glaze/topping (optional, see pages 162–3)

Pour the water and oil into the breadmaker bucket, followed by the salt, sugar, cheese and chives. Cover with the flour and sprinkle the yeast over. Fit the bucket into the breadmaker and set to the French programme. Once cooked, carefully shake the loaf from the bucket and stand the right way up on a wire cooling rack. Brush with your chosen glaze and add any topping (if using). Leave the bread to cool for at least an hour before cutting and/or removing the paddle if necessary.

Home-made Breads
For All Occasions

For Breakfast and Brunch

CHOCOLATE AND HAZELNUT BREAD

This is one of my favourite sweet bread recipes and I was in a quandary as to where if fitted best in the book. However, when I was engrossed in testing recipes, the bread neatly found its niche as the best accompaniment to mid-morning coffee. For added variety, try this recipe with other nuts such as walnuts and pecans.

200 ml/7 fl oz/^{7}/$_8$ cup semi-skimmed milk

3 tbsp melted butter, cooled

1 large egg, beaten

1^1/$_2$ tsp sugar

1 tsp salt

450 g/16 oz/3 cups very strong white bread flour

1^1/$_4$ tsp instant or fast-acting dried yeast

75 g/3 oz/^{3}/$_8$ cup chocolate chips

50 g/2 oz/^{3}/$_8$ cup chopped toasted hazelnuts

glaze/topping (optional, see pages 162–3)

Pour the milk into the breadmaker bucket, followed by the butter and egg. Add the sugar and salt. Cover with the flour and sprinkle the yeast over. Fit the bucket into the breadmaker and set to the basic white programme. Add the chocolate chips and nuts according to your manual's instructions, usually at the beginning or the middle of the second kneading cycle or when the machine bleeps. Once cooked, carefully shake the loaf from the bucket and stand the right way up on a wire cooling rack. Brush with your chosen glaze and add any topping (if using). Leave the bread to cool for at least an hour before cutting and/or removing the paddle if necessary.

BANANA AND OAT BREAKFAST BREAD

This moist, wonderfully aromatic loaf has just the right amount of texture for a wholesome breakfast bread. Sliced, it makes great toast. As the moisture content of bananas varies enormously I'd advise checking the dough during the second kneading cycle and making any necessary adjustments; the dough should be moist but not runny.

125 ml/4 fl oz/½ cup water

1 large egg, beaten

2 tbsp vegetable oil

2 tsp salt

2 tbsp demerara sugar

3 ripe bananas, puréed or mashed

100 g/3½ oz/1 cup jumbo oats

225 g/8 oz/1½ cups soft grain strong white bread flour

225 g/8 oz/1½ cups strong white bread flour

1¼ tsp instant or fast-acting dried yeast

glaze/topping (optional, see pages 162–3)

Pour the water into the breadmaker bucket, followed by the egg, oil, salt, sugar and bananas. Top with the oats and flour. Finally, sprinkle the yeast over. Fit the bucket into the breadmaker and set to the basic white programme. If you prefer a crusty loaf and have an adjustable crust setting on your machine, set it to dark. Once cooked, carefully shake the loaf from the bucket and stand the right way up on a wire cooling rack. Brush with your chosen glaze and add any topping (if using). Leave the bread to cool for at least an hour before cutting and/or removing the paddle if necessary.

CINNAMON BREAD WITH QUINOA AND DATES

With the fantastic aroma that this loaf gives off while cooking it'll be hard to let it cool before eating it! This wonderfully aromatic bread with the nutritious boost of quinoa (see page 16) is perfect for breakfast or brunch, either served with butter or as the base for French Toast (see page 50).

150 ml/5 fl oz/⅝ cup semi-skimmed milk

150 ml/5 fl oz/⅝ cup water

2 tbsp melted butter, cooled

3 tbsp maple syrup

2½ tsp ground cinnamon

1½ tsp salt

50 g/1 oz/½ cup quinoa flakes

450 g/16 oz/3 cups very strong white bread flour

1½ tsp instant or fast-acting dried yeast

75 g/3 oz/⅝ cup roughly chopped dates

glaze/topping (optional, see pages 162–3)

Pour the milk, water, butter and syrup into the breadmaker bucket, followed by the cinnamon and salt. Cover the wet ingredients with the quinoa flakes and flour and finally sprinkle the yeast over. Fit the bucket into the breadmaker and set to the basic white programme. Add the dates according to your manual's instructions, usually at the beginning or the middle of the second kneading cycle or when the machine bleeps. Once cooked, carefully shake the loaf from the bucket and stand the right way up on a wire cooling rack. Brush with your chosen glaze and add any topping (if using). Leave the bread to cool for at least an hour before slicing and/or removing the paddle if necessary.

FRENCH TOAST

You can use any bread to make this French Toast recipe, but I especially like it when made with Cinnamon Bread with Quinoa and Dates (see page 49).

1 large egg
225 ml/8 fl oz/1 cup
semi-skimmed milk
2 tsp runny honey
1/4 tsp ground cinnamon
butter, for frying
4 slices of Cinnamon
Bread with Quinoa and
Dates

Makes 4 large slices

Beat the egg in a bowl and whisk in the milk, honey and cinnamon. Pour the mixture into a shallow dish. Heat a frying pan and when hot add some butter. Dip the slices in the egg mixture one at a time for a few seconds on each side. Fry in the butter until crisp and golden on both sides, wiping out the pan with kitchen towel between each slice to remove any residue. Serve the toast immediately with maple syrup and/or more butter.

BREAKFAST MILK LOAF

This close-textured loaf has a light golden crust and makes the most wonderful toast. Made with milk, it's particularly good for those children who insist on eating only white bread.

225 ml/8 fl oz/1 cup plus
2 tbsp semi-skimmed milk
1 1/2 tsp sugar
1 1/2 tsp salt
450 g/16 oz/3 cups
strong white bread flour
1 1/4 tsp instant or fast-
acting dried yeast
glaze/topping (optional,
see pages 162–3)

Pour the milk into the breadmaker bucket and add the sugar and salt. Cover with the flour and sprinkle the yeast over. Fit the bucket into the breadmaker and set to the basic white programme. Once cooked, carefully shake the loaf from the bucket and stand the right way up on a wire cooling rack. Brush with your chosen glaze and add any topping (if using). Leave the bread to cool for at least an hour before cutting and/or removing the paddle if necessary.

French Toast

For Lunchtime, Picnics and Sandwiches

FRENCH BREAD BRUSCHETTA

I'm mad about sun-ripened tomatoes and love fresh coriander too, so is it any surprise that I'm hooked on Australia's version of bruschetta? Bruschetta is simply an Italian version of toast and, while the elements for this recipe are largely the same as we have in UK restaurants, I enjoyed this all over Australia as a full meal rather than a dainty starter. Piled high with the chunky tomato salsa, this really is summer on a plate. So, in memory of sunny days, here's my recipe for the Aussie bruschetta.

FOR THE TOPPING

8 large, good-quality ripe tomatoes, peeled and seeded

1 small red onion, peeled and finely chopped

1 clove of garlic, crushed

3 heaped tbsp chopped fresh coriander

salt and freshly ground black pepper

FOR THE BRUSCHETTA

4 slices of French Garlic and Herb Bread (see page 39)

olive oil, for drizzling

1 large clove of garlic

Serves 2

Preheat the oven to 225°C/425°F/gas mark 7.

Cut the tomato flesh into 5 mm/¼ in dice and place in a bowl with the onion, garlic and coriander. Season well, stir and leave to stand while you make the bruschetta.

Halve the bread slices diagonally and place on a baking sheet. Drizzle with the olive oil and immediately place in the hot oven. Bake for 10–15 minutes until crisp, checking every few minutes. Rub the bruschetta with the garlic clove while still warm, then place on a serving plate. Cover with the tomato mixture and serve immediately.

GREEN TEA AND PINE NUT BREAD

So many of us rely on sandwiches for our weekday lunch, so why not make them extra special with this wonderfully versatile bread? Encapsulating the goodness of green tea and the added crunch of pine nuts, this loaf will complement any sandwich filling.

250 ml/9 fl oz/1⅛ cups very strong green tea, at room temperature

2½ tbsp sunflower oil

2½ tbsp runny honey

1 tsp salt

450 g/16 oz/3 cups strong brown bread flour

1½ tsp instant or fast-acting dried yeast

75 g/3 oz/½ cup pine nuts, lightly toasted

glaze/topping (optional, see pages 162–3)

Pour the tea and oil into the breadmaker bucket, followed by the honey and salt. Cover with the flour and sprinkle the yeast over. Fit the bucket into the breadmaker and set to the basic white programme. Add the pine nuts according to your manual's instructions, usually at the beginning or the middle of the second kneading cycle or when the machine bleeps. Once cooked, carefully shake the loaf from the bucket and stand the right way up on a wire cooling rack. Brush with your chosen glaze and add any topping (if using). Leave the bread to cool for at least an hour before cutting and/or removing the paddle if necessary.

BRIE AND REDCURRANT LOAF

Whether served alongside a Sunday roast or at lunchtime the following day for sandwiches made with the leftover cold meat, this tasty bread is a real winner. The classic combination of Brie and redcurrant jelly translates wonderfully into bread, giving a rich, moist loaf worthy of any occasion.

150 ml/5 fl oz/⅝ cup water

1 large egg, beaten

3 tbsp redcurrant jelly

1 tsp salt

125 g/4 oz/1 cup crumbled ripe Brie

100 g/3½ oz/¾ cup country grain strong brown bread flour

100 g/3½ oz/¾ cup strong wholemeal bread flour

225 g/8 oz/1½ cups very strong white bread flour

1½ tsp instant or fast-acting dried yeast

glaze/topping (optional, see pages 162–3)

Pour the water into the breadmaker bucket, add the egg, then the redcurrant jelly and salt. Add the Brie and cover with the flours. Finally, sprinkle the yeast over. Fit the bucket into the breadmaker and set to the wholewheat or wholemeal rapid programme. Once cooked, carefully shake the loaf from the bucket and stand the right way up on a wire cooling rack. Brush with your chosen glaze and add any topping (if using). Leave the bread to cool for at least an hour before cutting and/or removing the paddle if necessary.

OLIVE BREAD

This light and airy loaf is the perfect accompaniment to salad and pasta dishes. It's my favourite bread to accompany a creamy carbonara or a fresh niçoise salad. When made with finely chopped olives, I frequently use it to make crunchy croutons for Caesar Salad (see below). It's also excellent served with a bowl of really good extra virgin olive oil for dipping as part of the starter for an informal supper party.

275 ml/10 fl oz/1¼ cups water

2 tbsp olive oil, plus extra for glazing

2 tsp sugar

1½ tsp salt

450 g/16 oz/3 cups very strong white bread flour

1¼ tsp instant or fast-acting dried yeast

60 g/2¼ oz/½ cup green or black olives, chopped

Pour the water and oil into the breadmaker bucket, followed by the sugar and salt. Cover with the flour and sprinkle the yeast over. Fit the bucket into the breadmaker and set to the basic white programme. Add the olives according to your manual's instructions, usually at the beginning or the middle of the second kneading cycle or when the machine bleeps. Once cooked, carefully shake the loaf from the bucket and stand the right way up on a wire cooling rack. Glaze by brushing with olive oil and leave to cool for at least an hour before slicing and/or removing the paddle if necessary.

CAESAR SALAD WITH CROUTONS

3 slices of Olive Bread, crusts removed

4 tbsp sunflower oil

4 slices of streaky bacon or 16 anchovy fillets

2 romaine lettuce hearts, washed and drained

20 pitted black olives

8 tbsp Caesar salad dressing

20 shavings taken from a piece of Parmesan cheese with a potato peeler

freshly ground black pepper (optional)

Serves 4

Cut the bread slices into chunky dice. Heat the oil in a frying pan until very hot, add the bread and fry until crispy on all sides. Drain on kitchen paper. Remove the rind from the bacon (if using). Cook under a hot grill, then drain on kitchen paper and cut into strips. Tear the lettuce into pieces and use to line a large serving plate. Sprinkle the bacon or anchovies and the olives over. Drizzle with the dressing and top with the Parmesan shavings. Finally sprinkle the croutons over, add a good grounding of pepper, if using, and serve immediately.

TORTINO

This wonderful filled focaccia bread is perfect for picnics and packed lunches. The herb dough, rich with olive oil, is filled with tomatoes, onions and olives.

FOR THE TOMATO SAUCE

3 tbsp olive oil

1 large onion, chopped

3 tsp dried oregano

2 cloves of garlic, crushed

1 x 400 g/14 oz can chopped tomatoes in juice

4 tbsp tomato purée

salt and freshly ground black pepper

60 g/2¼ oz/½ cup pitted green or black olives, halved

FOR THE DOUGH

200 ml/7 fl oz/⁷/₈ cup water

75 ml/3 fl oz/³/₈ cup olive oil, plus extra for brushing

1½ tsp salt

1½ tsp sugar

2 tsp mixed dried herbs (optional)

450 g/16 oz/3 cups very strong white bread flour

2½ tsp instant or fast-acting dried yeast

sea salt and fresh rosemary sprigs, to top (optional)

To make the tomato sauce, heat the oil in a large frying pan and add the onion and oregano. Cook over a low heat until the onion is soft and translucent (do not let it brown). Add the garlic, tomatoes and tomato purée and season with salt and pepper. Stir well and leave the sauce for about 15–20 minutes to reduce over a low heat until it has thickened. Leave to cool completely, then stir in the olives.

To make the dough, pour the water and oil into the breadmaker bucket and add the salt, sugar and herbs (if using). Cover with the flour and sprinkle the yeast over. Fit the bucket into the breadmaker and set to the dough programme.

When the cycle is complete, turn the dough out on to a floured surface and knead until smooth. Divide the dough in half and roll out both pieces into equal-sized rounds about the diameter of a dinner plate. Transfer one round to a greased baking sheet and cover with the cool tomato sauce, keeping the sauce away from the edges as you would for a pizza. Brush the dough around the edge with water and carefully place the second round of dough on top, pressing the edges together to seal. Take care to ensure the edge is completely sealed so the sauce does not leak out during cooking. Cover with a tea towel and leave to prove until springy to the touch. Using your fingertips carefully dimple the top of the dough, taking care not to puncture it, and brush with olive oil. Sprinkle with sea salt and stud with the rosemary sprigs (if using). Bake in a preheated oven at 200°C/400°F/gas mark 6 for 30–35 minutes. Brush again with olive oil while still warm and leave to cool on a wire rack. Serve warm or cold.

VARIATION: Omit the olives from the tomato sauce and add 100 g/3½ oz/ 1 cup sliced button mushrooms with the tomatoes.

NEW YORK STREET POTATO PIZZA

I first ate this pizza out of paper walking around New York in the snow doing my Christmas shopping. Buying such a tasty treat from a simple street stand was an unexpected pleasure and a sublime experience on a cold December day. This pizza has a great combination of flavours, making it perfect for lunch with a crisp salad or as part of a buffet for a party. It's also delicious served cold, making it a useful dish for picnics.

FOR THE DOUGH

250 ml/9 fl oz/1 1/8 cups water

50 ml/2 fl oz/1/4 cup olive oil

1 1/2 tsp sugar

1 1/2 tsp salt

450 g/16 oz/3 cups strong white bread flour

2 1/2 tsp instant or fast-acting dried yeast

FOR THE TOPPING

5 medium potatoes

1 tbsp sea salt

1 large red onion, peeled, sliced and separated into rings

fresh rosemary sprigs, chopped

freshly ground black pepper

3 tbsp olive oil, plus extra for brushing

flour, for dusting

Makes 2 large pizzas
Serves 8–10

To make the dough, pour the water and oil into the breadmaker bucket and add the sugar and salt. Cover with the flour and sprinkle the yeast over. Fit the bucket into the breadmaker and set to the dough programme.

About half an hour before the dough is ready prepare the topping. Peel the potatoes and slice them as thinly as possible (paper-thin slices made with a food processor or mandolin are best). Put the slices in a bowl and toss in the salt, then leave them to exude their liquid for about 15 minutes. Squeeze them dry and then combine with the onion slices and rosemary. Season with plenty of black pepper.

When the dough cycle is complete, turn the dough out on to a lightly floured surface and knead until smooth. Divide the dough in half and roll each piece into a round large enough to cover a 30 cm/12 in oiled and flour-dusted pizza tin, gently pulling and stretching the dough until it reaches the edges of the tin. Brush the dough with olive oil and cover with the potato mixture to within 2.5 cm/1 in of the edges. Finish with more black pepper and a drizzle of olive oil. Bake at 220°C/425°F/gas mark 7 for 20–30 minutes. Serve hot.

NOTE: for a pizza with a thicker crust, leave the dough to prove before topping with the potato slices.

For Barbecues and Suppers

GRAIN MUSTARD AND BEER BREAD

Whether you're serving up a hearty casserole or looking for the perfect bread to go with a barbecued steak, what could be better than this rich, tasty loaf enhanced with grain mustard and peppered with mustard seeds?

225 ml/8 fl oz/1 cup flat beer

4 tbsp sunflower oil

2 tbsp grain mustard

2$^1\!/_2$ tbsp runny honey

1$^1\!/_2$ tsp salt

100 g/3$^1\!/_2$ oz/$^3\!/_4$ cup strong wholemeal bread flour

100 g/3$^1\!/_2$ oz/$^3\!/_4$ cup rye flour

2 tbsp black mustard seeds

225 g/8 oz/1$^1\!/_2$ cups very strong white bread flour

2$^1\!/_2$ tsp instant or fast-acting dried yeast

glaze/topping (optional, see pages 162–3)

Pour the beer into the breadmaker bucket, followed by the oil, mustard, honey and salt. Cover with the wholemeal and rye flours. Sprinkle the mustard seeds over and top with the white flour and finally the yeast. Fit the bucket into the breadmaker and set to the wholewheat or rapid programme. Once cooked, carefully shake the loaf from the bucket and stand the right way up on a wire cooling rack. Brush with your chosen glaze and add any topping (if using). Leave the bread to cool for at least an hour before cutting and/or removing the paddle if necessary.

WHOLEMEAL SOURED CREAM BREAD WITH HERBS

The perfect loaf for any dinner party. Subtle yet flavoursome, this bread is versatile enough to complement any menu. It's especially good served as a starter with pâté or smoked salmon. I like to present it cut into wide triangular wedges.

125 ml/4 fl oz/¹/₂ cup water

150 ml/5 fl oz/⁵/₈ cup soured cream

1 large egg, beaten

1 tbsp sunflower oil

1 tbsp sugar

1 tsp salt

1 tsp dried rosemary

1 tsp dried thyme

225 g/8 oz/1¹/₂ cups strong brown bread flour

100 g/3¹/₂ oz/³/₄ cup strong wholemeal bread flour

100 g/3¹/₂ oz/³/₄ cup very strong white bread flour

1¹/₂ tsp instant or fast-acting dried yeast

glaze/topping (optional, see pages 162–3)

Pour the water and cream into the breadmaker bucket, followed by the egg, oil, sugar and salt. Add the herbs and the flours and finally sprinkle the yeast over. Fit the bucket into the breadmaker and set to the basic white programme. Once cooked, carefully shake the loaf from the bucket and stand the right way up on a wire cooling rack. Brush with your chosen glaze and add any topping (if using). Leave the bread to cool for at least an hour before slicing and removing the paddle if necessary.

PARMESAN AND SUNDRIED TOMATO BREAD

No breadmaking book would be complete without a sundried tomato bread and as this recipe includes Parmesan cheese it combines two of today's favourite bread flavourings. Unlimited in its uses, this loaf is wonderful with all Mediterranean dishes. I love it with a crisp summer salad served with continental hams and salami or alongside a creamy wild mushroom risotto.

250 ml/9 fl oz/1⅛ cups water

25 ml/1 fl oz/⅛ cup olive oil

1 tbsp sugar

2 tsp salt

70 g/2½ oz/½ cup soft grain strong white bread flour

70 g/2½ oz/½ cup rye flour

30 g/1¼ oz/½ cup finely grated Parmesan cheese

300 g/11 oz/2 cups strong white bread flour

1¼ tsp instant or fast-acting dried yeast

50 g/2 oz/½ cup roughly chopped sundried tomatoes

glaze/topping (optional, see pages 162–3)

Pour the water and oil into the breadmaker bucket, followed by the sugar and salt. Add the soft grain flour and then the rye flour. Sprinkle the Parmesan over and cover with the strong white bread flour. Finally, sprinkle the yeast over. Fit the bucket into the breadmaker and set to the basic white programme. Add the tomatoes according to your manual's instructions, usually at the beginning or the middle of the second kneading cycle or when the machine bleeps. Once cooked, carefully shake the loaf from the bucket and stand the right way up on a wire cooling rack. Brush with your chosen glaze and add any topping (if using). Leave the bread to cool for at least an hour before cutting and/or removing the paddle if necessary.

DOUBLE PEPPER BREAD

A light, airy bread with just the right amount of kick from the black pepper and fresh green peppercorns. It's one of my favourite breads to go with soup and also excellent for barbecues, where it adds a special touch.

275 ml/10 fl oz/1¼ cups water

1½ tbsp sunflower oil

1 egg yolk

1 tbsp sugar

2 tsp salt

1 tsp ground black pepper

70 g/2½ oz/½ cup strong wholemeal bread flour

375 g/13 oz/2½ cups strong white bread flour

1¼ tsp instant or fast-acting dried yeast

3 tbsp fresh green peppercorns

glaze/topping (optional, see pages 162–3)

Pour the water and oil into the breadmaker bucket, followed by the egg yolk, sugar, salt and black pepper. Cover with the flours and sprinkle the yeast over. Fit the bucket into the breadmaker and set to the basic white programme. Add the green peppercorns according to your manual's instructions, usually at the beginning or the middle of the second kneading cycle or when the machine bleeps. Once cooked, carefully shake the loaf from the bucket and stand the right way up on a wire cooling rack. Brush with your chosen glaze and add any topping (if using). Leave the bread to cool for at least an hour before slicing and removing the paddle if necessary.

TURKISH FLATBREADS

These flatbreads are quick to prepare and make a sophisticated lunch (also see page 64).

300 ml/11 fl oz/1³/₈ cups water

2 tbsp olive oil

1 tsp salt

1 tsp sugar

450 g/16 oz/3 cups strong white bread flour

2 tsp instant or fast-acting dried yeast

Egg wash (see page 163)

poppy seeds

Makes 2 flatbreads

Pour the water and olive oil into the breadmaker bucket, followed by the salt and sugar. Cover with the flour and sprinkle the yeast over. Fit the bucket into the breadmaker and set to the dough programme. When the cycle is complete, turn the dough out on to a lightly floured surface and knead until smooth. Divide the dough in half and shape each piece into a ball. Roll out each dough ball into a large round about 1 cm/½ in thick. Transfer the flatbreads to greased baking sheets, cover with a tea towel and leave to prove for 20 minutes. Brush with egg wash and sprinkle with poppy seeds. Bake at 220°C/425°F/gas mark 7 for 10–12 minutes until puffy and golden.

TURKISH FLATBREADS WITH SPICY LAMB AND TZATZIKI

450 g/1 lb boned leg of lamb

FOR THE MARINADE

2 tbsp olive oil

grated rind of 1 lemon

2 tbsp lemon juice

1 tsp ground cumin

1 tsp ground coriander

1/2 tsp ground tumeric

1/2 tsp paprika

1 clove of garlic, crushed

1 tsp harissa paste

1 small red chilli, seeded and finely chopped (optional)

freshly ground black pepper

FOR THE TZATZIKI

1/4 cucumber

1 tsp sea salt

125 ml/4 fl oz/1/2 cup natural yoghurt

2 tbsp chopped fresh mint leaves

1 clove of garlic, crushed

1 tsp chopped fresh oregano

a pinch of caster sugar

juice of 1 lime

freshly milled black pepper, to taste

2 Turkish Flatbreads (see page 63)

Serves 2

Cut the lamb into strips about 1 cm/1/2 in wide and 4 cm/11/2 in long. Combine all the marinade ingredients in a large bowl and add the lamb, stirring until it's all well covered. Cover the bowl with clingfilm and leave in the fridge for at least 2 hours or even overnight to allow the flavours to penetrate the meat.

Make the tzatziki just before you cook the meat. Dice the cucumber and toss in a bowl with the sea salt. Transfer to a sieve over a bowl and leave for 5–10 minutes to allow the cucumber to exude its excess water. Towards the end of this time you can lightly press the cucumber to squeeze any water out, but take care not to crush it. In a separate bowl combine the yoghurt, mint, garlic, oregano, sugar and lime juice. Add the cucumber, stir well and season with black pepper to taste.

Cook the marinated meat for 10–15 minutes either in a griddle pan, on the barbecue or in the oven at 220°C/425°F/gas mark 7.

To serve, warm the Turkish Flatbreads, top with the spicy lamb and serve with the tzatziki and a crisp salad.

FOCACCINI

These little focaccia breads are excellent served with any barbecue or alfresco meal. They're perfect with gazpacho, delicious with pâté and excellent topped with roasted or barbecued vegetables. See my recipe below for Roasted Vegetable Focaccini.

200 ml/7 fl oz/⅞ cup water

75 ml/3 fl oz/⅜ cup olive oil, plus extra for brushing

1½ tsp salt

1½ tsp sugar

2 tsp dried oregano

450 g/16 oz/3 cups very strong white bread flour

2½ tsp instant or fast-acting dried yeast

Makes 4

Pour the water and olive oil into the breadmaker bucket, followed by the salt, sugar and oregano. Cover with the flour and sprinkle the yeast over. Fit the bucket in the breadmaker and set to the dough programme. When the cycle is complete, turn the dough out on to a floured surface and knead until smooth. Divide the dough into quarters and roll each piece into a round about 1 cm/½ in thick. Place the rounds on greased baking sheets, cover with a tea towel and leave to prove until doubled in size. Using your fingertips, dimple the top of the dough, brush with olive oil and bake in a preheated oven 200°C/400°F/gas mark 6 for 10–15 minutes. Transfer to the cooling rack and brush again with olive oil while still warm.

ROASTED VEGETABLE FOCACCINI

1 red pepper, sliced

1 yellow pepper, sliced

1 red onion, sliced

2 cloves of garlic, sliced

1 courgette, halved and sliced

12 cherry tomatoes, halved

3 tbsp olive oil, plus extra for drizzling

4 Focaccini breads (above)

salt and freshly ground black pepper

16 slices of Mozzarella cheese

basil leaves, to garnish

Serves 4

Mix together the vegetables in a bowl. Heat a griddle on the hob or on the barbecue until very hot, then pour in the olive oil. Add the vegetables and cook until soft and nicely charred (you could also do this in a hot oven). While the vegetables are cooking, warm the focaccinis in the oven or on top of the barbecue. Cover the breads with the roasted vegetables, season well and arrange the Mozzarella slices on top. Place the breads on the barbecue or under the grill until the cheese is melted. Garnish with basil leaves and serve immediately drizzled with olive oil.

Roasted Vegetable Focaccini

For Dessert and Tea Time

BASIC SWEET BREAD

Here's a basic sweet dough recipe that you can use to make a vast range of sweet teatime breads. I've listed some of my favourite additions for flavouring this dough (see page 70); you may like to try these or some of your own.

125 ml/4 fl oz/½ cup
semi-skimmed milk

125 ml/4 fl oz/½ cup
water

1 large egg yolk

3 tbsp melted butter,
cooled

4 tbsp sugar

1 tsp salt

450 g/16 oz/3 cups
strong white bread flour

1¼ tsp instant or fast-
acting dried yeast

flavourings of your
choice (see below)

glaze/topping (optional,
see pages 162–3)

Pour the milk and water into the breadmaker bucket, then add the egg, butter, sugar and salt. Cover with the flour and sprinkle the yeast over. Fit the bucket into the breadmaker and set to the basic white programme. Add any fruit or nuts (see page 70) according to the manual's instructions, usually at the beginning or middle of the second kneading cycle or when the machine bleeps. When ready, carefully shake the loaf out of the bucket and stand the right way up on a wire cooling rack. Brush with your chosen glaze and add any topping (if using). Leave for at least an hour before cutting and/or removing the paddle if necessary.

BLUEBERRY, PECAN AND MAPLE BREAD

Follow the recipe for Basic Sweet Bread (see page 68), replacing the sugar with 4 tbsp maple syrup. Add 75 g/3 oz/1/2 cup semi-dried blueberries and 50 g/2 oz/1/2 cup roughly chopped pecan nuts as directed in the recipe.

DATE AND WALNUT BREAD

Follow the recipe for Basic Sweet Bread (see page 68), adding 2 tsp ground mixed spice before the flour and 50 g/2 oz/1/2 cup roughly chopped walnuts and 75 g/3 oz/5/8 cup chopped dates as directed in the recipe.

SPICED APPLE AND CINNAMON LOAF

Follow the recipe for Basic Sweet Bread (see page 68), adding 2 tsp ground cinnamon before the flour and 125 g/4 oz/3/4 cup roughly chopped semi-dried apple as directed in the recipe.

Blueberry, Pecan and Maple Bread

COCONUT AND ORANGE TEA BREAD

A truly luxurious bread, perfect for tea time. The rich flavours of fresh orange, liqueur and coconut are sublime in this beautifully moist bread. It needs nothing more than butter.

200 ml/7 fl oz/⁷/₈ cup creamed coconut

50 ml/2 fl oz/¹/₄ cup water

50 ml/2 fl oz/¹/₄ cup orange juice

50 ml/2 fl oz/¹/₄ cup orange liqueur, e.g. Cointreau

1 tsp salt

1 tsp sugar

grated rind of 2 oranges

50 g/2 oz/¹/₂ cup desiccated coconut

450 g/16 oz/3 cups strong white bread flour

2¹/₂ tsp instant or fast-acting dried yeast

glaze/topping (optional, see pages 162–3)

Pour the coconut cream, water, orange juice and orange liqueur into the breadmaker bucket. Add the salt, sugar, orange rind and desiccated coconut. Cover with the flour and sprinkle the yeast over. Fit the bucket into the breadmaker and set to the basic white programme. When cooked, carefully shake the loaf from the bucket and stand the right way up on a cooling rack. Brush with your chosen glaze and add any topping (if using). Leave the loaf for at least and hour before cutting and/or removing the paddle if necessary.

PRUNE AND CHOCOLATE BREAD

Succulent prunes and rich chocolate – the perfect combination. Need I say more?

200 ml/7 fl oz/⁷/₈ cup semi-skimmed milk

3 tbsp melted butter, cooled

1 large egg, beaten

1¹/₂ tsp sugar

1 tsp salt

450 g/16 oz/3 cups strong white bread flour

1¹/₄ tsp instant or fast-acting dried yeast

75 g/3 oz/³/₈ cup chocolate chips

125 g/4 oz/³/₄ cup ready-to-eat prunes, halved

glaze/topping (optional, see pages 162–3)

Pour the milk into the breadmaker bucket, followed by the butter and egg. Add the sugar, salt, then the flour and finally sprinkle the yeast over. Fit the bucket into the breadmaker and set to the basic white programme. Add the chocolate chips and the prunes according to the manual's instructions, usually at the beginning or middle of the second kneading cycle or when the machine bleeps. Once cooked, carefully shake the loaf out of the bucket and stand the right way up on a wire cooling rack. Brush with your chosen glaze and add any topping (if using). Leave for at least an hour before cutting and/or removing the paddle if necessary.

SAFFRON BRIOCHE

This light and airy brioche can be baked on a full breadmaker cycle. The richly fragranced loaf is easily sliced, making it the perfect base for this delicious variation of a classic pudding. Saffron Brioche Bread and Butter Pudding makes an impressive, yet simple, dinner party dessert.

2 tbsp milk

1/2 tsp saffron strands

3 large eggs, beaten

6 tbsp water

125 ml/4 fl oz/1/2 cup melted butter, cooled

2 tbsp sugar

1/2 tsp salt

450 g/16 oz/3 cups strong white bread flour

2 1/2 tsp instant or fast-acting dried yeast

melted butter, to glaze

Heat the milk until just scalded. Stir in the saffron strands and leave to cool.

To make the brioche, pour the milk and saffron infusion into the breadmaker bucket, followed by the eggs, water, butter, sugar and salt. Cover the liquid with the flour and finally sprinkle the yeast over. Fit the bucket in the breadmaker and set to the basic white programme. When ready, carefully shake the loaf from the bucket and stand the right way up on a wire cooling rack. Brush the warm loaf with melted butter, then leave for at least an hour before cutting and/or removing the paddle if necessary.

BREAD AND BUTTER PUDDING

8 slices of Saffron Brioche (see above), crusts removed

butter, for spreading and greasing

50 g/2 oz/1/4 cup sultanas

3 large eggs

275 ml/10 fl oz/1 1/4 cups full cream milk

75 ml/3 fl oz/3/8 cup double cream

50 g/2 oz/1/4 cup caster sugar

Butter the slices of brioche and cut each slice into four triangles. Grease a 1 litre/2 pint/4 3/4 cup oven-proof dish and arrange the triangles in layers in the dish, sprinkling in the sultanas in between the layers and finishing with a final layer of bread without any fruit on top. In a bowl, whisk together the eggs, milk, cream and sugar. Pour this mixture over the bread and, if you have time, leave the pudding to stand in the fridge for an hour to allow the brioche to soak up the cream mixture.

Preheat the oven to 180°C/350°F/gas mark 4 and place the dish in a roasting tray three-quarters filled with warm water. Put the whole lot in the oven for about 30–40 minutes until the pudding is just firm. Remove from the oven and serve warm. For an extra crisp topping, sprinkle the baked pudding with a couple of teaspoons of caster sugar and glaze under a medium grill until the sugar has caramelised.

Bread and Butter Pudding

DARK CHOCOLATE BREAD

A chocoholic's dream. Despite the rich chocolate flavour of this bread, friends of mine have still plastered it with chocolate and hazelnut spread. One thing is for sure, it will never go to waste, so if you want to make Chocolate Biscotti (recipe below) to accompany a soufflé, mousse or chocolate fondue, you'll have to keep this loaf hidden away.

350 ml/12 fl oz/1½ cups semi-skimmed milk

1½ tbsp melted butter

75 g/3 oz/¾ cup good quality plain chocolate, melted and allowed to cool slightly

2 tbsp sugar

1 tsp salt

50 g/2 oz/³⁄₈ cup cocoa powder

450 g/16 oz/3 cups very strong white bread flour

1¼ tsp instant or fast-acting dried yeast

glaze/topping (optional, see pages 162–3)

Pour the milk into the breadmaker bucket, followed by the butter and chocolate. Add the sugar, salt and cocoa powder and cover with the flour. Finally, sprinkle the yeast over. Fit the bucket into the breadmaker and set to the sweet or rapid programme. Once cooked, carefully shake the loaf from the bucket and stand the right way up on a wire cooling rack. Brush with your chosen glaze and add any topping (if using). Leave the bread to cool for at least an hour before cutting and/or removing the paddle if necessary.

CHOCOLATE BISCOTTI

Little chocolate biscotti fingers are an excellent crunchy treat with a chocolate mousse, or simply serve them after dinner with coffee. For an extra special touch the ends of each can be dipped in melted chocolate after cooking.

To make biscotti, simply cut 1 cm/½ in slices from a loaf of Dark Chocolate Bread, remove the crusts and cut into fingers, or into any shape with a biscuit cutter. Preheat the oven to 180°C/350°F/gas mark 4. Arrange the biscotti on a baking tray and bake for 20 minutes or until crisp, turning over half-way through the cooking time. Transfer to a wire rack and leave to cool.

APPLE STREUSEL KÜCHEN

The first time I served this was at a lunch party where my guests' children were highly amused that they had 'pizza' for pudding. But they say the proof of the pudding is in the eating and it certainly was here. With a dough lightly flavoured with cinnamon, smothered with tart apples and topped with a crisp streusel topping, who could resist? It's perfect accompanied with thick double cream, even clotted cream. I serve it hot for the meal and any leftovers always make the perfect snack the following day. For an alternative presentation, try making individual küchen in a bun tin – they're excellent finger food for a party.

FOR THE APPLE MIXTURE

4 medium cooking apples, peeled, cored and diced

50 ml/2 fl oz/¼ cup water

3 tbsp sugar

FOR THE DOUGH

200 ml/7 fl oz/⅞ cup milk, plus extra for brushing

1 large egg, beaten

2 tbsp melted butter, cooled

2 tbsp sugar

1 tsp salt

1 tsp ground cinnamon

450 g/16 oz/3 cups strong white bread flour

1¼ tsp instant or fast-acting dried yeast

FOR THE TOPPING

100 g/3½ oz/¼ cup butter

100 g/3½ oz/¾ cup plain flour

50 g/2 oz/¼ cup demerara sugar

Makes 1 large or 2 small küchen

To make the apple mixture, cook the apples in the water until just soft. Stir in the sugar and set aside to cool.

To make the dough, pour the milk into the breadmaker bucket, followed by the egg and butter. Add the sugar and salt, then sprinkle the cinnamon and flour over. Finally, add the yeast. Fit the bucket into the breadmaker and set to the dough programme. When the cycle is complete, turn the dough out on to a lightly floured surface and knead until smooth. Roll the dough into a round or rounds about 5 mm/¼ in thick. Brush the edges of the dough with milk, then cover with the cooled apple.

To make the streusel topping, rub the butter into the flour until it resembles breadcrumbs. Stir in the sugar. Sprinkle the topping over the apple. Cover the küchen with a tea towel and leave in a warm place for 20 minutes. Bake in a preheated oven at 200°C/400°F/gas mark 6 for 20–30 minutes. Serve hot.

For Special Occasions

PANNETONE

This beautifully rich bread is light, fragrant and moist. Every time I've made this recipe it's disappeared very quickly, which is always the sign of a real winner. In fact, although this is traditionally a Christmas bread, once tasted you'll be serving it all year round.

2 medium egg yolks

150 ml/5 fl oz/5/8 cup milk

75 ml/3 fl oz/3/8 cup water

3 tbsp melted butter, cooled

1 tsp vanilla extract

1 tbsp granulated sugar

1 tsp salt

grated zest of 1 orange

grated zest of 1 lemon

pinch of freshly grated nutmeg

450 g/16 oz/3 cups very strong white bread flour

1 1/4 tsp instant or fast-acting dried yeast

50 g/2 oz/1/4 cup sultanas

25 g/1 oz/1/8 cup mixed peel

glaze/topping (optional, see pages 162–3)

Pour the egg yolks, milk, water, butter and vanilla extract into the breadmaker bucket. Put the sugar to one side and the salt to the other, then add the grated orange and lemon zest and the nutmeg. Cover the wet ingredients with the flour, make a well in the centre and sprinkle in the yeast. Set the machine to the basic white programme. Add the sultanas and mixed peel according to your manual's instructions, usually at the beginning or middle of the second kneading cycle or when the machine bleeps. When cooked, carefully shake the loaf from the bucket and stand the right way up on a wire cooling rack. If liked, brush with your selected glaze. Leave the bread to cool for at least an hour before slicing and/or removing the paddle if necessary.

BREADMAKER STOLLEN

I experimented over Christmas with many different stollen recipes; some with dough wrapped around a marzipan filling and some with either grated marzipan or almonds added. This is my version and I think it encapsulates the best from all of the recipes I tested, giving a fragrant loaf that can be baked on a complete cycle, which is more convenient at the most hectic time of year. As the dough is heavily laden with fruit, spices and alcohol, a good dose of yeast is needed to produce this dense, yet soft-textured bread. Remove the loaf carefully from the bucket and let it cool completely before slicing. Serve simply sliced with butter and jam or try it toasted for breakfast.

100 g/3½ oz/¾ cup raisins

50 g/2 oz/¼ cup currants

25 g/1 oz/³∕₈ cup flaked almonds

½ tsp ground cardamom seeds

¼ tsp freshly grated nutmeg

a pinch of finely ground black pepper

zest and juice of 1 lemon

½ tsp vanilla extract

2 tbsp rum

225 ml/8 fl oz/1 cup milk

100 g/3½ oz/½ cup very soft butter

100 g/3½ oz/⅝ cup finely chopped marzipan

½ tsp salt

4 tbsp granulated sugar

450 g/16 oz/3 cups strong white bread flour

3 tsp instant or fast-acting dried yeast

glaze/topping (optional, see pages 162–3)

Put the raisins, currants, almonds, spices and pepper in a bowl. Pour the lemon zest and juice, the vanilla extract and rum over. Stir and leave for at least 2 hours to allow the fruit to soak up the flavours.

To make the stollen, pour the milk into the breadmaker bucket, followed by the fruit mixture, the butter, marzipan, salt and sugar. Top with the flour and finally sprinkle the yeast over. Fit the bucket into the breadmaker and set to the normal/basic white programme. Once cooked, carefully shake the loaf from the bucket and stand the right way up on a wire cooling rack. Brush with your chosen glaze and add any topping (if using). Leave the bread to cool for at least an hour before cutting and/or removing the paddle if necessary.

KÜGELHOPF

In Austria sweet kügelhopf loaded with fruit is traditionally served for special occasions. In recent years savoury versions have come to the fore and this is my breadmaker adaptation – still a rich bread but flavoured with bacon, onion, herbs and cheese. Quite delicious.

125 ml/4 fl oz/½ cup water plus 1½ tbsp

2 medium eggs, beaten

2 tbsp melted butter, cooled

1 tsp sugar

1 tsp salt

2 rashers of bacon, cooked and chopped

2 tbsp dried onion flakes

¾ tsp dried or fresh thyme

½ tsp ground black pepper

75 g/3 oz/1 cup grated Swiss cheese

450 g/16 oz/3 cups strong white bread flour

1¼ tsp instant or fast-acting dried yeast

glaze/topping (optional, see pages 162–3)

Pour the water into the breadmaker bucket, followed by the eggs and butter. Add the sugar, salt, bacon, onion, thyme, pepper and cheese. Cover with the flour and sprinkle the yeast over. Fit the bucket into the breadmaker and set to the basic white programme. Once cooked, carefully shake the loaf from the bucket and stand the right way up on a wire cooling rack. Brush with your chosen glaze and add any topping (if using). Leave the bread to cool for at least an hour before cutting and/or removing the paddle if necessary.

Sourdough Made Easy

Sourdough Made Easy

Making bread using a starter is a wonderful way of getting an even wider variety of loaves from your breadmaker. While I would not recommend these as the first breads the complete novice should make, they're certainly worth a go if you're a more experienced bread machine owner.

Starters have been used for centuries to create the distinctive flavour and texture of many breads from all round the world, the most famous of which is undoubtedly San Francisco sourdough. Starters are also commonly used in many continental recipes; the French call them a *poolish* and the Italians a *biga* and, though the preparation method and fermentation time may vary, the ingredients themselves remain the same. Some artisan bakers guard their starter recipe fiercely as it is the secret ingredient for their particular loaves.

The recipes in this section are perfect if you like your bread to have that slightly yeasty, sour aroma and a rich flavour, and the recipes in this chapter open the door to a whole new realm of possibilities where taste and flavour are concerned. To guide your through the complexities of using a starter, I've first included breads made using a simple overnight sponge. While a little pre-planning is required for these, it only takes a couple of minutes to mix the starter and, once the fermentation is complete, your bread will take no longer than normal to prepare. I think you'll agree that using starters will add a whole new dimension to your breadmaking repertoire.

The flavour of a starter can be varied to your taste by using different liquids and flours; rye flour and wholemeal flours can be used and the liquid chosen could be buttermilk or even flat beer.

Traditionally a sourdough starter is made from flour and water only. This is then left to ferment using the natural yeast from the grain itself and also the wild yeasts present in the air. To have a starter powerful enough for the regulated breadmaker cycle, I've had to cheat slightly by creating the starter initially with a little dried yeast. I've found it far more practicable to speed up the fermentation process in this way, and then to let the flavour develop naturally over time as the starter matures.

For those trying to cut down on manufactured yeast in their diets, breadmaking with a starter can be an excellent option. Although a starter may use a little manufactured yeast to get it going, as it is refreshed time after time and allowed to mature, the proportion will reduce as it's replaced by natural yeast, making this a potentially useful option for some special diets. Of course there's nothing to stop you experimenting with the traditional sourdough starter using no added yeast, but for best results in a breadmaker you'll need to use the dough cycle only and then let your bread prove slowly until doubled in size. The loaf can then be cooked either on the bake cycle or in the oven.

The length of time a starter is left to mature is very much a matter of taste. Basically, the longer you keep your starter the stronger the 'sour' flavour of the bread. French *poolish* ferments for at least 2 hours to give a less yeasty taste; the Italian *biga* is generally left for at least 12 hours; and rustic sourdough breads are usually made from a starter

that has fermented for at least 48 hours to give a pleasant sour aroma and flavour, a hearty texture and chewy crust. Once you've tried the recipes in this chapter a few times you'll be able to experiment further by letting your starter mature to suit your personal taste.

Making bread with a starter using traditional methods is easier than in a breadmaker as the dough can be left to rise until doubled in size without any limitation on time. In a breadmaker, where rising times are strictly controlled, it can be a little more erratic; for your particular machine

you may have to adjust the recipe slightly. I'm sure you'll agree that the extra time and effort involved in making bread with a starter will be well worthwhile, allowing you to discover a whole new range of breads with superior taste and texture.

The first recipes in this chapter are the quickest and easiest to prepare as they use a simple overnight sponge that you add to the mix the next morning. Following these, I've moved on to more complex recipes based on my sourdough-style starter.

Breads Made With an Overnight 'Sponge' Starter

CORN BREAD

Moist, light and airy with the added sweetness of corn, this is a wonderful, warming, rich yellow bread.

FOR THE OVERNIGHT SPONGE

150 g/5¼ oz/1 cup strong white bread flour

¾ tsp instant or fast-acting dried yeast

175 ml/6 fl oz/¾ cup warm water

TO FINISH THE BREAD

150 ml/5 fl oz/⅝ cup warm water

1 medium egg, beaten

1½ tbsp olive oil

150 g/5¼ oz/¾ cup sweetcorn kernels

190 g/6½ oz/1 cup instant polenta

2 tbsp runny honey

300 g/11 oz/2 cups strong white bread flour

2 tsp salt

1 tsp instant or fast-acting dried yeast

glaze/topping (optional, see pages 162–3)

To make the sponge, mix together the ingredients to form a thick batter. Cover with a tea towel and leave to ferment overnight (or for 8–12 hours).

When you are ready to make the bread, pour the water into the breadmaker bucket, followed by the egg, oil, sweetcorn and fermented overnight sponge. Cover with the polenta and then add the honey. Finally, add the flour. Put the salt to one side and the yeast to the other side on top of the flour. Fit the bucket into the breadmaker and set to the basic white programme. When cooked, carefully shake the loaf from the bucket and stand the right way up on a wire cooling rack. Brush with your chosen glaze and add any topping (if using). Leave the bread to cool for at least an hour before cutting and/or removing the paddle if necessary.

GERMAN COUNTRY BREAD WITH CARAWAY SEEDS

Anyone who has visited Germany and experienced the true wonders of their fantastic breads will be more than willing to try recreating the wonderful flavours and textures at home. This beautifully aromatic loaf is rich and wholesome, making it the perfect partner for a cold meat buffet or a hearty stew.

FOR THE OVERNIGHT SPONGE

50 g/2 oz/7 tbsp strong white bread flour

½ tsp instant or fast-acting dried yeast

3 tbsp water

1 tbsp milk

TO FINISH THE BREAD

250 ml/9 fl oz/1⅛ cups water

2 tbsp caraway seeds

225 g/8 oz/1½ cups rye flour

2 tsp salt

2 tbsp sugar

225 g/8 oz/1½ cups very strong white bread flour

1¼ tsp instant or fast-acting dried yeast

glaze/topping (optional, see pages 162–3)

To make the sponge, mix together the ingredients to form a smooth paste. Cover with a tea towel and leave to ferment overnight (or for 8–12 hours).

When you are ready to make the bread, pour the water into the breadmaker bucket, followed by the fermented overnight sponge. Add the caraway seeds and cover with the rye flour. Add the salt, sugar and then the white flour. Finally, sprinkle the yeast over. Fit the bucket into the breadmaker and set to the rapid/wholemeal rapid programme. Once cooked, carefully shake the loaf from the bucket and stand the right way up on a wire cooling rack. Brush with your chosen glaze and add any topping (if using). Leave the bread to cool for at least an hour before cutting and/or removing the paddle if necessary.

WALNUT BREAD

This delicious walnut bread is perfect with any meal and is really excellent served with cheese. The overnight sponge adds a special dimension to the taste, making this a truly sophisticated bread.

FOR THE OVERNIGHT SPONGE

100 g/3½ oz/¾ cup strong wholemeal bread flour

1 tsp runny honey

1 tsp instant or fast-acting dried yeast

125 ml/4 fl oz/½ cup water

TO FINISH THE BREAD

225 ml/8 fl oz/1 cup water

2 tbsp walnut oil

150 g/5¼ oz/1 cup strong wholemeal flour

1 tbsp runny honey

2 tsp salt

250 g/9 oz/1¾ cups very strong white bread flour

1¼ tsp instant or fast-acting dried yeast

100 g/3½ oz/1 cup roughly chopped walnuts

glaze/topping (optional, see pages 162–3)

To make the sponge, mix together the ingredients to form a thick batter. Cover with a tea towel and leave to ferment overnight (or for 8–12 hours).

When you are ready to make the bread, pour the water into the breadmaker bucket, followed by the fermented overnight sponge. Add the oil and cover with the wholemeal flour. Next add the honey, salt and then the white flour. Finally, sprinkle the yeast over. Fit the bucket into the breadmaker and set to the basic white programme. Add the walnuts according to your manual's instructions, usually at the beginning or middle of the second kneading cycle or when the machine bleeps. Once cooked, carefully shake the loaf from the bucket and stand the right way up on a wire cooling rack. Brush with your chosen glaze and add any topping (if using). Leave the bread to cool for at least an hour before cutting and/or removing the paddle if necessary.

SALT-FREE ITALIAN BREAD

This is my breadmaker adaptation of the traditional Tuscan bread, which was developed when a heavy salt tax in the Middle Ages encouraged the Tuscans to develop bread recipes without salt. With a crisp crust and a soft airy centre, this is a pleasing bread that's perfect for mopping up the juices of a fine Bolognese sauce. While no salt is great news for many of today's special diets, it also means that this bread will not keep, so enjoy it on the day that it's baked.

Making bread without salt is a tricky business in a breadmaker as salt controls the action of the yeast, so in your particular model this recipe may need a little trial and error to achieve a good crust. Make sure you measure the ingredients very carefully when making this loaf.

FOR THE OVERNIGHT SPONGE

150 g/5$\frac{1}{4}$ oz/1 cup very strong white bread flour

1$\frac{1}{4}$ tsp instant or fast-acting dried yeast

125 ml/4 fl oz/$\frac{1}{2}$ cup water

TO FINISH THE BREAD

200 ml/7 fl oz/$\frac{7}{8}$ cup water

300 g/11 oz/2 cups very strong white bread flour

1 tsp sugar

To make the sponge, mix together the ingredients to form a sticky dough. Cover with a tea towel and leave to ferment overnight (or for 8–12 hours).

When you are ready to make the bread, pour the water into the breadmaker bucket, followed by the fermented overnight sponge. Add the flour and the sugar. Fit the bucket into the breadmaker and set to the French programme. Once cooked, carefully shake the loaf from the bucket and stand the right way up on a wire cooling rack. Leave the bread to cool for at least an hour before cutting and/or removing the paddle if necessary.

SEMOLINA BREAD

This wonderful, light and airy loaf has a crisp yet chewy crust and a warm yellowish interior. It's delicious served in chunks with soft, runny cheese and is perfect with pâté. Make the most of this irresistible bread by eating it fresh on the day it's baked.

FOR THE OVERNIGHT
SPONGE

125 g/4 oz/⁷/₈ cup very
strong white bread flour

¹/₄ tsp instant or fast-
acting dried yeast

150 ml/5 fl oz/⁵/₈ cup
water

TO FINISH THE BREAD

175 ml/6 fl oz/³/₄ cup
water

4 tbsp olive oil

250 g/9 oz/1³/₈ cups
semolina

2 tsp salt

2 tbsp sugar

150 g/5¹/₄ oz/1 cup
very strong white bread
flour

2 tsp instant or fast-
acting dried yeast

glaze/topping (optional,
see pages 162–3)

To make the sponge, mix together the ingredients to form a smooth, thick batter. Cover with a tea towel and leave to ferment overnight (or for 8-12 hours).

When you are ready to make the bread, pour the water and oil into the breadmaker bucket, followed by the fermented overnight sponge. Cover with the semolina and then the salt, sugar and flour. Finally, sprinkle the yeast over. Fit the bucket into the breadmaker and set to the basic white programme. Once cooked, carefully shake the loaf from the bucket and stand the right way up on a wire cooling rack. Brush with your chosen glaze and add any topping (if using). Leave the bread to cool for at least an hour before cutting and/or removing the paddle if necessary.

Breads Made With a Sourdough-Style Starter

All the breads that follow in this chapter are made using my Sourdough-style Starter. This starter will need to be made and refreshed if you are going to make loaves with it on an ongoing basis. I find making bread in this way both rewarding and enjoyable; you get all the convenience of using the breadmaker and the chance to utilise a traditional method of leavening bread with a home-made natural starter – it's the best of both worlds.

SOURDOUGH-STYLE STARTER

300 ml/11 fl oz/1³/₈ cups water

250 g/9 oz/1³/₄ cups strong white bread flour

2 tsp instant or fast-acting dried yeast

Mix together all the ingredients and cover with a tea towel. Leave to ferment at room temperature for at least 3 days to a maximum of 5 days. During this time the starter will become a loose, frothy batter. After the required fermentation time, cover with clingfilm and store in the fridge. Before using, stir the mixture and let it come slowly to room temperature. The starter should be slightly frothy and pleasantly sour smelling.

TO REPLENISH YOUR STARTER:

When you have used some of the starter it should be replenished by adding the equivalent amount of flour and water in equal quantities. For example, if the recipe requires 225 ml/8 fl oz/1 cup of starter, stir in 125 ml/4 fl oz/¹/₂ cup water and 125 g/4 oz/⁷/₈ cup flour. Allow the starter to ferment again at room temperature for 24 hours, then cover with clingfilm and return it to the fridge until needed. There is no need to add more yeast, as a mature starter makes its own natural yeast; by adding flour and moisture you are supplying the ingredients it needs to multiply, ensuring it is of suitable strength for the next time it is needed.

Once made, this starter can be kept in the fridge indefinitely as long as it is refreshed at least once every two weeks. To refresh a starter, stir it, discard half and replenish with equal quantities of water and flour and proceed as above. If you bake regularly, this process will happen naturally as you remove some starter for your loaf and add fresh water and flour to replace it.

BREADMAKER SOURDOUGH

Moist and rich, this is a wonderful sourdough-style loaf.

275 ml/10 fl oz/1¼ cups Sourdough-style Starter (see page 92)

150 ml/5 fl oz/⅝ cup water

2 tbsp sunflower oil

70 g/2½ oz/½ cup strong wholemeal flour

375 g/13 oz/2½ cups very strong white bread flour

1½ tsp salt

2 tsp sugar

glaze/topping (optional, see pages 162–3)

Pour the starter, water and oil into the breadmaker bucket. Cover with the flours and sprinkle on the salt and sugar. Fit the bucket into the breadmaker and set to the basic white programme. When cooked, carefully shake the loaf from the bucket and stand the right way up on a wire cooling rack. Brush with your chosen glaze and add any topping (if using). Leave the bread to cool for at least an hour before slicing and/or removing the paddle if necessary.

CIABATTA

Remember the word ciabatta means 'slipper', so don't be too fussy when shaping this dough – it's supposed to be rough and irregular in appearance.

125 ml/4 fl oz/½ cup Sourdough-style Starter (see page 92)

275 ml/10 fl oz/1¼ cups water

3 tbsp olive oil

3 tbsp rye flour

450 g/16 oz/3 cups very strong white bread flour, plus extra for dusting

1½ tsp salt

2 tsp sugar

1¼ tsp instant or fast-acting dried yeast

Pour the starter into the breadmaker bucket, followed by the water and oil. Cover the liquid with the rye flour and half the white flour. Sprinkle the salt and sugar over and cover with the remaining flour. Finally, sprinkle the yeast over. Fit the bucket into the breadmaker and set to the dough programme. When the cycle is complete, turn the dough out on to a lightly floured surface and divide in half. Stretch each half into a rough round about the size of a dinner plate and then fold roughly like an envelope to give the traditional ciabatta shape. Place each loaf on an oiled baking sheet and cover with a tea towel. Leave to prove until risen and springy to the touch. Dust with flour and bake in a preheated oven 200°C/400°F/gas mark 6 for 15–20 minutes. When cooked, transfer to a wire cooling rack and leave to cool.

ROASTED GARLIC BREAD

When roasted, garlic takes on a beautifully sweet taste and the harshness of its raw flavour is lost. This bread makes the most of this wonderful flavour by rolling puréed roasted garlic into the dough and then returning it to the breadmaker for baking.

FOR THE ROASTED GARLIC

1 whole head of garlic

1 tbsp olive oil

salt and freshly ground black pepper

TO FINISH THE BREAD

175 ml/6 fl oz/³/₄ cup water

275 ml/10 fl oz/1¹/₄ cups Sourdough-style Starter (see page 92)

450 g/16 oz/3 cups very strong white bread flour

1 tbsp runny honey

2 tsp salt

glaze/topping (optional, see pages 162–3)

To roast the garlic, preheat the oven to 190°C/375°F/gas mark 5. Slice the top off the head of garlic so that the inside of the cloves is just exposed. Place the garlic head on a large enough piece of foil to enclose it completely. Pour the olive oil over and season with salt and pepper. Wrap in the foil and roast in the oven for 1 hour. When cooked, allow the garlic to cool and then split the bulb and squeeze the soft garlic purée from each clove. Discard the skin and root part of the bulb. Mash the garlic in a bowl together with any juices from the foil. Cool, cover with clingfilm and reserve until needed.

When ready to make the bread, pour the water into the breadmaker bucket, followed by the starter. Cover with the flour and top with the honey and salt. Fit the bucket into the breadmaker and set to the dough programme. When the cycle is complete, turn the dough out on to a lightly floured board and roll out to a square approximately 30 cm/12 in across. Spread the dough with the garlic purée. Fold in the left and right hand edges of the dough so that the dough is the same length as your breadmaker bucket, then roll up like a Swiss roll and place the bread back in the clean bucket. Leave to prove slowly until doubled in size (this will take longer than with a traditional yeast dough), then fit the bucket into the breadmaker and set to the bake programme. When cooked, carefully shake the loaf from the bucket and stand the right way up on a wire cooling rack. Brush with your chosen glaze and add any topping (if using). Leave the bread to cool for at least an hour before cutting and/or removing the paddle if necessary.

Artisan Baking

Inspiration for the following recipes comes from my good friend Dan De Gustibus, an award-winning artisan baker and owner of the De Gustibus bakeries and cafés in London. Dan makes some seriously good bread and I'm delighted to have adapted some of his classic recipes for this chapter. We are both firm believers in giving bread time to rise, so to do this within the limits of a breadmaker programme I've used the French bread setting for most of the breads made with a starter as this tends to be the cycle with the longest proving time. If you'd like to give your loaves even more time to rise naturally, you can use the dough programme, then shape, prove and bake the loaves in the traditional way.

SAN FRANCISCO SOURDOUGH

My breadmaker version of this classic sourdough bread.

275 ml/10 fl oz/1¼ cups Sourdough-style Starter (see page 92)

125 ml/4 fl oz/½ cup natural yoghurt

75 ml/3 fl oz/³⁄₈ cup water

2 tbsp sunflower oil

4½ tbsp strong wholemeal flour

4½ tbsp rye flour

2 tbsp honey

1½ tsp salt

375 g/13 oz/2½ cups very strong white bread flour

glaze/topping (optional, see pages 162–3)

Pour the starter, yoghurt and water into the breadmaker bucket and add the oil. Cover with the wholemeal and rye flours, then add the honey and salt. Finally, add the white bread flour. Fit the bucket into the breadmaker and set to the French programme. When cooked, carefully shake the loaf from the bucket and stand the right way up on a wire cooling rack. Brush with your chosen glaze and add any topping (if using). Leave the bread to cool for at least an hour before slicing and/or removing the paddle if necessary.

HERB-SCENTED PORCINI MUSHROOM BREAD

The rich flavour of porcini mushrooms enhanced with home-made herb-scented oil make this loaf as aromatic as it is flavoursome. It's my favourite choice to serve with a good Italian ragu sauce and pasta.

25 g/1 oz/1 cup dried porcini mushrooms

225 ml/8 fl oz/1 cup boiling water

3 tbsp olive oil

6–8 fresh sage leaves

3 bay leaves, sliced

225 ml/8 fl oz/1 cup Sourdough-style Starter (see page 92)

70 g/2½ oz/½ cup strong wholemeal flour

70 g/2½ oz/½ cup rye flour

300 g/11 oz/2 cups very strong white bread flour

2 tbsp runny honey

1½ tsp salt

glaze/topping (optional, see pages 162–3)

Soak the mushrooms in the boiling water for 30 minutes. Drain well, reserving the liquid, and finely chop the mushrooms. Heat the oil in a pan and gently fry the sage and bay leaves for 5 minutes. Turn off the heat and leave to infuse for 20 minutes.

When both the oil and mushrooms have cooled, prepare the bread. Drain the oil from the herbs into the breadmaker bucket. Discard the fried herbs. Add the mushroom stock and soaked mushrooms. Pour in the starter and cover with the flours. Finally, add the honey and salt. Fit the bucket into the breadmaker and set to the French programme. When cooked, carefully shake the loaf from the bucket and stand the right way up on a wire cooling rack. Brush with your chosen glaze and add any topping (if using). Leave the bread to cool for at least an hour before slicing and/or removing the paddle.

CRANBERRY BRIOCHE WITH BRIE

With the rich flavour and airy texture of a true brioche, this versatile recipe can be made in a complete breadmaker cycle. If you prefer the traditional shape, you can use the dough cycle and then shape the brioche. Either way you'll love the delicious combination of the subtle Brie and rich, juicy cranberries.

350 ml/12 fl oz/1½ cups Sourdough-style Starter (see page 92)

5 tbsp melted butter, cooled ·

2 large eggs, beaten

125 g/4 oz/1 cup diced ripe Brie

400 g/14 oz/2¾ cups very strong white bread flour

3 tbsp runny honey

1½ tsp salt

75 g/3 oz/½ cup ready-to-eat (semi-dried) cranberries

glaze/topping (optional, see pages 162–3)

Pour the starter into the breadmaker bucket, followed by the butter, eggs and Brie. Cover with the flour and add the honey and salt. Fit the bucket into the breadmaker and set to the French programme. Add the cranberries according to your manual's instructions, usually at the beginning or middle of the second kneading cycle or when the machine bleeps. When cooked, carefully shake the loaf from the bucket and stand the right way up on a wire cooling rack. Brush with your chosen glaze and add any topping (if using). Leave the bread to cool for at least an hour before slicing and/or removing the paddle.

WHOLEWHEAT CHESTNUT BREAD

This moist loaf builds on the natural sweetness of roasted chestnuts and creamy chestnut purée to give a versatile loaf that's excellent with roasted meat and rich casseroles.

100 g/3½ oz canned chestnuts

300 ml/11 fl oz/1³/₈ cups Sourdough-style Starter (see page 92)

200 g/7 oz/⁷/₈ cup canned chestnut purée

1 tbsp groundnut oil

25 ml/1 fl oz/⅛ cup water

375 g/13 oz/1½ cups very strong white bread flour

2 tsp salt

2 tsp sugar

glaze/topping (optional, see pages 162–3)

Roast the canned chestnuts in the oven at 200°C/400°F/gas mark 6 for about 10–15 minutes until just browned and fragrant. Watch them like a hawk so they don't over-brown and burn. Allow to cool, then slice.

Pour the starter into the breadmaker bucket followed by the chestnut purée, oil and water. Add the roasted chestnut slices and cover with the flour. Finally, add the salt and sugar. Fit the bucket into the breadmaker and set to the French programme. When cooked, carefully shake the loaf from the bucket and stand the right way up on a wire cooling rack. Brush with your chosen glaze and add any topping (if using). Leave the bread to cool for at least an hour before slicing and/or removing the paddle.

WILD RICE AND LENTIL SOURDOUGH BREAD

Wild rice and puy lentils balanced with the full sourdough flavour. A beautiful, moist loaf that is as sophisticated in appearance as it is in taste.

225 ml/8 fl oz/1 cup Sourdough-style Starter (see page 92)

125 ml/4 fl oz/½ cup water

3 tbsp natural yoghurt

2 tbsp groundnut oil

75 g/3 oz/½ cup cooked puy lentils

50 g/2 oz/³∕₈ cup cooked wild rice

70 g/2½ oz/½ cup rye flour

375 g/13 oz/2½ cups very strong white bread flour

2 tbsp runny honey

2 tsp salt

glaze/topping (optional, see pages 162–3)

Pour the starter, water, yoghurt and oil into the breadmaker bucket, followed by the lentils and rice. Cover with the flours and finally add the honey and salt. Fit the bucket into the breadmaker and set to the French programme. When cooked, carefully shake the loaf from the bucket and stand the right way up on a wire cooling rack. Brush with your chosen glaze and add any topping (if using). Leave the bread to cool for at least an hour before slicing and/or removing the paddle if necessary.

FIG AND ROSEMARY SOURDOUGH BREAD

A real taste of the Mediterranean. A light, moist loaf flavoured with fresh rosemary and sweetened with figs. It's delicious with cheese and cold meats.

275 ml/10 fl oz/1¼ cups Sourdough-style Starter (see page 92)

225 ml/8 fl oz/1 cup water

3 tbsp olive oil

4½ tbsp strong wholemeal bread flour

400 g/14 oz/2¾ cups very strong white bread flour

3 tbsp runny honey

1½ tsp salt

1½ tbsp chopped fresh rosemary

125 g/4 oz/¾ cup roughly chopped ready-to-eat figs

glaze/topping (optional, see pages 162–3)

Pour the starter, water and oil into the breadmaker bucket. Cover with the flours, then add the honey, salt and rosemary. Fit the bucket into the breadmaker and set to the French programme. Add the figs according to your manual's instructions, usually at the beginning or middle of the second kneading cycle or when the machine bleeps. When cooked, carefully shake the loaf from the bucket and stand the right way up on a wire cooling rack. Brush with your chosen glaze and add any topping (if using). Leave the bread to cool for at least an hour before slicing and/or removing the paddle if necessary.

COURGETTE AND CHEESE SOUR BREAD

In this scrumptious bread Dan combines full-flavoured cheese with succulent courgette and fragrant oregano.

125 ml/4 fl oz/½ cup water

225 ml/8 fl oz/1 cup Sourdough-style Starter (see page 92)

3 tbsp olive oil

100 g/3½ oz/1 cup finely diced courgette

75 g/3 oz/1 cup grated Cheddar cheese

2 tsp dried oregano

70 g/2½ oz/½ cup rye flour

2 tsp salt

2 tsp sugar

375 g/13 oz/2½ cups very strong white bread flour

glaze/topping (optional, see pages 162–3)

Pour the water, starter and oil into the breadmaker bucket, followed by the courgette, cheese and oregano. Cover with the rye flour then add the salt and sugar. Finally add the white bread flour. Fit the bucket into the breadmaker and set to the French programme. When cooked, carefully shake the loaf from the bucket and stand the right way up on a wire cooling rack. Brush with your chosen glaze and add any topping (if using). Leave the bread to cool for at least an hour before slicing and/or removing the paddle if necessary.

BUTTERMILK AND POTATO SOURDOUGH BREAD

Adding mashed potatoes makes a beautifully moist loaf. This base is then enhanced with a hint of cumin and the tangy flavour of the buttermilk and the starter. A versatile bread for any occasion.

275 ml/10 fl oz/1¼ cups Sourdough-style Starter (see page 92)

225 ml/8 fl oz/1 cup buttermilk

2 tbsp melted butter, cooled

225 g/8 oz/1 cup cold mashed potatoes

4½ tbsp rye flour

400 g/14 oz/2¾ cups very strong white bread flour

1½ tsp salt

2 tsp ground cumin

2 tbsp sugar

glaze/topping (optional, see pages 162–3)

Pour the starter, buttermilk and butter into the breadmaker bucket. Add the potato and cover with the flours. Finally, add the salt, cumin and sugar. Fit the bucket into the breadmaker and set to the French programme. When cooked, carefully shake the loaf from the bucket and stand the right way up on a wire cooling rack. Brush with your chosen glaze and add any topping (if using). Leave the bread to cool for at least an hour before slicing and/or removing the paddle if necessary.

Simple Solutions for Special Diets

Simple solutions for special diets

Think of the times you've heard phrases like 'bread – the staff of life', or even 'give us this day our daily bread'. Both lead us unmistakably to the fact that bread has been the core of our diets for thousands of years. But as science, medicine and society have become more sophisticated so has our knowledge of foods that can fight with our well-being. Consequently, in today's society it's commonplace to follow an exclusion diet – wheat-free, gluten-free, dairy-free – or, indeed, to have to eliminate some foods and maximise others to help manage an ongoing medical condition like heart disease or diabetes.

Whether through medical necessity or a concern for personal well-being, a change in your diet can be hard to manage. And, when this change seems to eliminate your toast at breakfast time, your sandwiches at lunchtime, and something to soak up your soup at suppertime, the situation can look bleak.

I've spoken to many people who have reached this point in their lives. They've called the Allinson helpline, desperate for a thread of hope on how bread, in some form, can still be part of their daily diet. And the truth is it can, albeit made with a different set of ingredients and maybe in a different way. By making bread yourself you have complete control over what goes into it and you can produce many breads that will allow toast and sandwiches to remain part of daily life.

With only a single chapter to devote to this subject I've focused on the key exclusion diets that are also applicable when trying to treat a host of other conditions. For example, dairy products are a common trigger for eczema and so the dairy-free breads will be useful for this condition. I've then demonstrated how certain key ingredients can be used in bread recipes to boost their nutritive value in a way that serves the demands of certain conditions or life-stages. The introductions to the recipes in this chapter explain how certain

ingredients used in the bread could help with the management of special diets and physical conditions, so you'll be able to decide which recipes are most suited to your personal needs. In addition, look out for the bulleted points under each recipe that indicate the value of each particular bread. The following dietary categories have been covered:

Exclusion Diets

WHEAT-FREE

For many a wheat-free diet may seem at first to eliminate completely the chance of ever eating bread again. However, with the wide choice of alternative flours available in supermarkets and health food stores and via the internet, there's a lot of scope for tasty alternatives. The main consideration here is that without the strong gluten structure provided by wheat, making loaves on a complete breadmaker cycle is not possible with some flours. However, there is nothing to stop you using the dough cycle and then letting the bread rise as normal and baking it in the oven.

The one exception is spelt. Although this grain is closely related to wheat, it has been found that many individuals who cannot tolerate wheat can, in fact, eat spelt. If in any doubt check with your

GP or dietician that spelt is suitable for your needs. If it is, then wheat-free breads on complete breadmaker cycles are a viable alternative. I have included several recipes using spelt in this chapter (see also All Spelt Bread on page 30). In addition, as the gluten-free recipes have to preclude wheat, these would also be relevant for a wheat-free diet.

GLUTEN-FREE
Gluten intolerance or coeliac disease is diagnosed in about 50,000 people in the UK, though it's estimated that a further 500,000 could have the condition without knowing it. For sufferers gluten affects the lining of the small intestine, producing symptoms ranging from abdominal discomfort and diarrhoea to prolonged tiredness and anaemia. Generally, the symptoms will disappear if a gluten-free diet is adopted.

A gluten-free diet means that grains like wheat, barley, spelt, kumat, rye and oats, and their products – bran, wheatgerm, semolina, durum, bulghar and couscous – must all be strictly avoided. Care should also be taken to avoid cross-contamination from utensils used for cooking wheat products and particular vigilance should be observed if your breadmaker is used for anything other than wheat- and gluten-free baking. It is also worth being meticulous in looking at labels to check the ingredients and investigating whether processed and manufactured foods or ingredients contain gluten. Either contact the supplier directly or obtain a copy of the Coeliac Society's list of gluten-free products (see page 171).

Despite the elimination of many grains, those on a coeliac diet can usually eat the following flours, which don't contain gluten: potato, rice, corn, buckwheat, tapioca, chickpea (channa), gram, millet, quinoa, soya and arrowroot, together with their products such as cornmeal and polenta.

DAIRY-FREE
A dairy-free diet can be needed either because of a lactose intolerance, where sufferers lack the enzyme lactase which breaks down lactose (milk sugar), or because of an allergy to the protein components of milk. Dairy foods are a well-known trigger for eczema, and many young children have an allergy to dairy products that they grow out of naturally as they mature. In addition to this, dairy-free diets can be chosen for many other reasons.

EGG-FREE
Some recipes in this book contain egg, but you can use a cholesterol-free egg substitute (available from health food shops), used in the recipes according to the manufacturer's instructions on the pack. Bulleted points are used to highlight recipes that do not include egg.

SUGAR-FREE
Sugar free and low-sugar diets are commonly followed to help with weight control and also in healthy eating regimes. Bread in itself is a relatively low-sugar food, so the first point to make is that you are probably better off cutting down the sugar contained in what you eat on it or with it, e.g. jam and marmalade.

I've used the minimum amount of sugar in recipes wherever possible within the limits of breadmaker cycles, and in some cases honey is used as a more natural alternative. In certain recipes in this chapter, processed sugar has been omitted completely and replaced with fruit juice concentrate or fruit juices. These recipes show you how these naturally sweet alternatives can be used in your everyday bread making.

YEAST-FREE

But yeast is needed to make bread, isn't it? Yes, it is. However, many people cannot tolerate manufactured yeast or are trying to at least cut down on it. If this is the case you can consider the yeast-free recipes in this chapter that are made using the quick bread or cake cycles of the breadmaker. Alternatively, for a longer-term solution you may like to consider experimenting with using a mature sourdough starter (see page 92). While your starter will have been created with a little manufactured yeast, over time, as it is refreshed with flour and water, the proportion of yeast of natural airborne origin to manufactured will increase. Breads made with a starter like this can be extremely helpful in some diets. As always, discuss your individual needs with your GP or dietitian before deciding on which is the best route for you.

HIGH-PROTEIN

Whether it's to fuel growth in children, to help during pregnancy or to assist in convalescence after an operation or illness, there are times in our lives when a high-protein diet is desirable. The simplest way to increase protein in bread, without simultaneously increasing the fat content with dairy products, is to use quinoa (see page 16) and I have developed many high-protein recipes using quinoa both in this chapter and elsewhere in the book.

LOW-SALT

Low-salt diets are usually recommended for the treatment of high blood pressure and, in general,

cutting down on salt added to food is relatively simple to do. In bread, however, it can be tricky as salt regulates the action of yeast. Ideally, it's best simply to cut salt to the minimum in bread rather than cutting it out completely. Remember, while a couple of teaspoons of salt may go into a loaf, a slice of bread will contain only a fraction of this. Using some salt is especially important when baking in a breadmaker, where the machine strictly regulates rising and proving times. Leaving out salt may lead to breads either rising out of control or falling in on themselves. For best results try turning your attention to cutting out the salt in what you put on the bread rather than in it.

In this book I have kept salt levels to a minimum and included a traditional Tuscan recipe for salt-free bread (see page 90).

HIGH-FIBRE

While eating a high fibre diet is something that is desirable for general good health, specific medical conditions such as constipation, diverticular disease and irritable bowel syndrome also require it. Many of the recipes in this book made with wholemeal flour and added grains are high in fibre and I have included recipes in this chapter with other added ingredients to boost the fibre content still further.

LOW-FAT

Cutting down on fat is probably one of the commonest dietary modifications made today. Remember that bread is not a high fat food in itself; it's usually what you put on it that makes the difference. However, for the benefit of those who want no added fat or oil in their loaves I've included relevant recipes in this chapter.

HIGH-CALCIUM

Calcium is vital for the growth and maintenance of healthy bones and teeth. Obviously children, teenagers and pregnant women all fall into the group needing a calcium-rich diet. But, as the body's ability to absorb calcium decreases with age, it's also an important nutrient for later life too and especially for women during and after the menopause.

HEALTHY HEART

Diet is a major part of the ongoing treatment of heart disease and its associated conditions – angina and high blood pressure. Primarily it's what you spread on bread that's the prime concern as saturated fats and cholesterol levels need to be closely monitored. Healthy heart recipes in this chapter use beneficial oils like canola oil and other advantageous ingredients like seeds and their oils, sweet potato and apricots which can all help with the total management of this condition.

MENOPAUSE MANAGEMENT

As a staple in the diet, bread can be a good source of additional nutrients commonly recommended to ease symptoms of the menopause. Calcium, magnesium, zinc and vitamins B and E are all important for this life stage. They are also nutrients valued for the treatment of PMS. Look for the bulleted points for breads that can assist these conditions.

DIABETES MANAGEMENT

Support groups for people with diabetes recommend eating regular meals based on starchy foods like bread to help control blood sugar levels. Guidelines are also given for

adopting a low-fat and low-added-sugar diet. The recipes for diabetes management in this chapter follow these basic principles and contain added ingredients that can also assist with this condition. As always with any medical condition, you should follow the instructions of your GP or dietitian for your particular requirements and adapt any recipes accordingly.

FENNEL TEA BREAD WITH YAM

Fennel and yam are key herbal remedies for the treatment of certain menopausal symptoms and they combine here to make this deliciously light and fragrant loaf.

Yams are an excellent source of magnesium, calcium, phosphorus and many vitamins. What's more, compounds in yam will bind to heavy metals in the body making them an excellent aid to detoxification. Working with fennel, this bread also offers potassium – a great regulator of blood pressure – and folic acid, which is essential in early pregnancy. The use of fennel tea is also valuable as it's famous for helping digestion.

225 ml/8 fl oz/1 cup strong fennel tea, cooled (or water)

2 tbsp sunflower oil

2 tbsp sugar

1½ tsp salt

2 tbsp fennel seeds

2 tbsp dried onion flakes

75 g/3 oz/½ cup cooked mashed yam, cooled

4½ tbsp rye flour

400 g/14 oz/2¾ cups very strong white bread flour

1¾ tsp instant or fast-acting dried yeast

glaze/topping (optional, see pages 162–3)

Pour the tea (or water) into the breadmaker bucket, followed by the oil, sugar and salt. Add the fennel seeds, onion flakes and yam. Cover the wet ingredients with the flours and sprinkle the yeast over. Fit the bucket into the breadmaker and set to the normal/basic white programme. Once cooked, carefully shake the loaf from the bucket and stand the right way up on a wire cooling rack. Brush with your chosen glaze and add any topping (if using). Leave the bread to cool for at least an hour before cutting and/or removing the paddle if necessary.

- *dairy-free*
- *healthy heart*
- *egg-free*
- *menopause management*

SWEET PEPPER BREAD WITH SMOKED PAPRIKA

A crispy crusted, wheat-free loaf punctuated with succulent pieces of pepper and enhanced with the rich taste of sweet smoked paprika. Needless to say it's wonderful with chilli dishes and also excellent with sausages and barbecued meats. The addition of red pepper also provides useful flavonoids that are said to help relieve the symptoms of allergy-related asthma.

225 ml/8 fl oz/1 cup water

2 tsp sweet smoked paprika

1/2 green pepper, seeded and chopped

1/2 red pepper, seeded and chopped

1/2 tsp salt

1 tbsp sugar

400 g/14 oz/2 3/4 cups spelt flour

4 1/2 tbsp gram flour

2 1/4 tsp instant or fast-acting dried yeast

glaze/topping (optional, see pages 162–3)

Pour the water into the breadmaker bucket, followed by the paprika, peppers, salt and sugar. Cover with the flours and sprinkle the yeast over. Fit the bucket into the breadmaker and set to the basic white programme. When cooked, carefully shake the loaf from the bucket and stand the right way up on a wire cooling rack. Brush with your chosen glaze and add any topping (if using). Leave the bread to cool for at least an hour before slicing and/or removing the paddle if necessary.

- *wheat-free*
- *egg-free*
- *low-fat*
- *dairy-free*
- *low-salt*
- *healthy heart*

CAJUN SPICED SOYA BREAD

Soy beans have seriously good health credentials. They are used here in three forms – as milk, as flour and as the key ingredient in tofu. For the healthy heart, soya contains antioxidants that help prevent damage to the artery walls and substances that prevent the blood from becoming sticky, thus helping prevent strokes and heart attacks. It's also said that soy proteins help lower LDL cholesterol. Some research even suggests that the genistein in soya beans appears to cut off the blood supply to cancer cells. This is echoed by research that suggests women who eat a diet rich in soya have lower rates of breast cancer, and men lower rates of prostate cancer. Soya also contains plant oestrogens called isoflavones that are well documented for helping to moderate the symptoms of the menopause and PMT.

Whether you're choosing this recipe for its health benefits or its taste, you won't be disappointed. This lightly spiced bread is fragrant, moist and speckled with onion, making it a delicious choice to accompany salads, cold meats and fish. You'll also love it as a base for really tasty sandwiches.

175 ml/6 fl oz/^{3}/$_4$ cup soya milk

2 tbsp canola oil

2 tbsp runny honey

1^1/$_4$ tsp salt

200 g/7 oz/1 cup finely diced silken tofu

50 g/2 oz/^{1}/$_2$ cup finely chopped red onion

1^1/$_2$ tsp Cajun spice

70 g/2^1/$_2$ oz/^{1}/$_2$ cup soya flour

190 g/6^1/$_2$ oz/1^1/$_4$ cups strong brown bread flour

190 g/6^1/$_2$ oz/1^1/$_4$ cups strong white bread flour

1^1/$_4$ tsp instant or fast-acting dried yeast

glaze/topping (optional, see pages 162–3)

Pour the soya milk into the breadmaker bucket, followed by the oil, honey and salt. Add the tofu, onion and spice. Cover the wet ingredients with the three flours and finally sprinkle the yeast over. Fit the bucket into the breadmaker and set to the normal/basic white programme. When cooked, carefully shake the loaf from the bucket and stand the right way up on a wire cooling rack. Brush with your chosen glaze and add any topping (if using). Leave the bread to cool for at least an hour before slicing and/or removing the paddle.

- *dairy-free*
- *egg-free*
- *high-protein*
- *menopause management*
- *healthy heart*

GREEN TEA AND LEMONGRASS BREAD

Subtly aromatic, this light, wheat-free loaf is perfect with Chinese and Thai dishes. The reputed benefits of green tea range from aiding digestion to helping prevent cancer. While the research is unproven, one thing is certain; green tea is high in antioxidants and using it as the liquid addition in bread is an excellent way of boosting the antioxidants in your diet.

225 ml/8 fl oz/1 cup strong green tea, at room temperature

2 tbsp lemongrass purée (from a jar)

1 tbsp sunflower oil

3/4 tsp salt

1 tbsp sugar

375 g/13 oz/2½ cups spelt flour

70 g/2½ oz/½ cup gram flour

2¼ tsp instant or fast-acting dried yeast

glaze/topping (optional, see pages 162–3)

Pour the green tea into the breadmaker bucket, followed by the lemongrass purée, oil, salt and sugar. Cover with the flours and sprinkle the yeast over. Fit the bucket into the breadmaker and set to the basic white programme. When cooked, carefully shake the loaf from the bucket and stand the right way up on a wire cooling rack. Brush with your chosen glaze and add any topping (if using). Leave the bread to cool for at least an hour before slicing and/or removing the paddle if necessary.

- *wheat-free*
- *dairy-free*
- *egg-free*

GLUTEN-FREE PESTO AND PEPPER BREAD

As this bread bakes your kitchen will be filled with the fragrance of a Mediterranean summer day, an aroma that is matched by the wonderful flavour of the bread. If you prefer, the gluten-free red pesto sauce can be substituted by gluten-free green pesto to vary the colour and flavour of the bread.

175 ml/6 fl oz/³/₄ cup water

150 ml/5 fl oz/⁵/₈ cup soya milk

1 tsp cider vinegar

1 large egg, beaten

50 ml/2 fl oz/¹/₄ cup sunflower oil

4 tbsp gluten-free red pesto sauce

1 red pepper, seeded and finely diced

1¹/₂ tbsp sugar

1¹/₂ tsp salt

450 g/16 oz/3 cups gluten-free bread flour

2¹/₂ tsp instant or fast-acting dried yeast

glaze/topping (optional, see pages 162–3)

Pour the water, soya milk, vinegar, egg and oil into the breadmaker bucket. Add the pesto, pepper, sugar and salt and cover with the flour. Finally, sprinkle the yeast over. Fit the bucket into the breadmaker and set to the gluten-free/quick bread or cake programme. Lift the lid of the machine as the dough is mixing and scrape down the sides of the bucket with a plastic spatula to ensure all the ingredients are incorporated into the dough. Once cooked, carefully shake the loaf from the bucket and stand the right way up on a wire cooling rack. Brush with your chosen glaze and add any topping (if using). Leave the bread to cool for at least an hour before cutting and/or removing the paddle if necessary.

- *wheat-free*
- *gluten-free*

GLUTEN-FREE WHITE BREAD

300 g/11 oz/2 cups rice flour

150 g/5¼ oz/1 cup potato starch (farina)

150 g/5¼ oz/1 cup tapioca flour

1 tbsp xanthum gum

1½ tsp salt

225 ml/8 fl oz/1 cup water

1 tsp cider vinegar

3 tbsp runny honey

125 ml/4 fl oz/½ cup beaten egg (approximately 2 large eggs)

50 ml/2 fl oz/¼ cup sunflower oil

125 ml/4 fl oz/½ cup rice milk

3 tsp instant or fast-acting dried yeast

Carefully measure the three flours into a bowl and add the xanthum gum and salt. Stir to blend all the ingredients together. Pour the water into the breadmaker bucket and add the vinegar, honey, eggs, oil and milk. Cover the liquid with the flour mixture and finally sprinkle the yeast over. Fit the bucket into the breadmaker and set to the gluten-free/quick bread or cake programme. Lift the lid of the machine as the dough is mixing and scrape down the sides of the bucket with a plastic spatula to ensure all the ingredients are incorporated into the dough. Once cooked, carefully shake the loaf from the bucket and stand the right way up on a wire cooling rack. Leave the bread to cool for at least an hour before cutting and/or removing the paddle if necessary.

- *wheat-free*
- *gluten-free*

MASCARPONE, ORANGE AND RAISIN TEA BREAD

Rich and fruity, this wonderful gluten-free loaf will be loved by everyone. In this delicious tea bread are hidden the benefits of calcium which, found in both the milk and cheese, work to strengthen bones and teeth, making this an excellent gluten-free choice for those who need these valuable nutrients.

190 g/6½ oz/1¼ cups rice flour

100 g/3½ oz/¾ cup potato starch

100 g/3½ oz/¾ cup tapioca flour

1 tbsp xanthum gum

1½ tsp salt

4 tbsp demerara sugar

100 g/3½ oz/¾ cup raisins

50 ml/2 fl oz/¼ cup water

1 tsp cider vinegar

2 large eggs, beaten

50 ml/2 fl oz/¼ cup melted butter, cooled

125 ml/4 fl oz/½ cup semi-skimmed milk

100 g/3½ oz/⅜ cup Mascarpone cheese

grated rind of 1 orange

75 ml/3 fl oz/⅜ cup fresh orange juice (juice of approximately 1 large orange)

3 tsp instant or fast-acting dried yeast

glaze/topping (optional, see pages 162–3)

In a bowl mix together the rice flour, potato starch, tapioca flour, xanthum gum, salt, sugar and raisins. Pour the water into the breadmaker bucket and add the vinegar, eggs, butter, milk, cheese, orange zest and juice. Cover with the flour mixture and finally sprinkle the yeast over. Fit the bucket into the breadmaker and set to the gluten-free/quick bread programme. Lift the lid of the machine as the dough is mixing and scrape down the sides of the bucket with a plastic spatula to ensure all the ingredients are incorporated into the dough. When cooked, carefully shake the loaf from the bucket and stand the right way up on a wire cooling rack. Brush with your chosen glaze and add any topping (if using). Leave to cool for at least an hour before slicing and/or removing the paddle if necessary.

- *wheat-free*
- *high-calcium*
- *gluten-free*

CHILLI CORN BREAD

Cornmeal is a wonderful gluten-free ingredient and it's used here to its best in this moist cornbread flavoured with chilli. Chillies are said to be good for asthma sufferers as they help desensitise the airways, while their mild irritant effect stimulates the stomach to defend itself against more serious bugs. In addition, this bread is a good source of fibre thanks to the cornmeal and sweetcorn. It's also rich in calcium from the yoghurt.

2 large eggs, beaten

425 ml/15 fl oz/1⁷⁄₈ cups natural yoghurt

50 ml/2 fl oz/¼ cup melted butter, cooled

200 g/7 oz/1³⁄₈ cups canned sweetcorn kernels, drained

2 red chillies, seeded and finely chopped

200 g/7 oz/1³⁄₈ cups gluten-free flour

250 g/9 oz/1³⁄₄ cups cornmeal

³⁄₄ tsp bicarbonate of soda

1½ tsp gluten-free baking powder

glaze/topping (optional, see pages 162–3)

Put the eggs, yoghurt, butter, sweetcorn and chilli in the breadmaker bucket. Cover with the flour, cornmeal, bicarbonate of soda and baking powder. Fit the bucket into the breadmaker and set to the gluten-free/quick bread or cake programme. Lift the lid of the machine as the dough is mixing and scrape down the sides of the bucket with a plastic spatula to ensure all the ingredients are incorporated into the dough. When cooked, carefully shake the loaf from the bucket and stand the right way up on a wire cooling rack. Brush with your chosen glaze and add any topping (if using). Leave to cool for at least an hour before slicing and/or removing the paddle if necessary.

- *wheat-free*
- *low-salt*
- *high-calcium*
- *yeast-free*
- *gluten-free*
- *high-fibre*
- *menopause management*

PARMESAN BREAD WITH OLIVES AND PUMPKIN SEEDS

This loaf is cleverly flavoured to make the perfect gluten-free accompaniment to Italian food and salads. Try using it for your favourite sandwich. The use of olives and olive oil follows the recommendations of the heart-healthy Mediterranean diet. Pumpkin seeds are rich in essential vitamins and minerals and have also been linked to helping alleviate prostate problems.

375 g/13 oz/2½ cups gluten-free white bread flour

70 g/2½ oz/½ cup gram flour

1 tsp xanthum gum

225 ml/8 fl oz/1 cup water

1 tsp cider vinegar

1 large egg, beaten

50 ml/2 fl oz/¼ cup olive oil

1½ tbsp runny honey

1½ tsp salt

25 g/1 oz/⅛ cup pumpkin seeds

50 g/2 oz/⅜ cup pitted green olives, sliced

50 g/2 oz/⅞ cup finely grated Parmesan cheese

3 tsp instant or fast-acting dried yeast

glaze/topping (optional, see pages 162–3)

In a bowl mix together the two flours and the xanthum gum. Pour the water into the breadmaker bucket followed by the vinegar, egg and oil. Add the honey, salt, pumpkin seeds, olives and cheese. Cover with the flour mixture and finally sprinkle the yeast over. Fit the bucket into the breadmaker and set to the gluten-free or quick bread programme. Lift the lid of the machine as the dough is mixing and scrape down the sides of the bucket with a plastic spatula to ensure all the ingredients are incorporated into the dough. When cooked, carefully shake the loaf from the bucket and stand the right way up on a wire cooling rack. Brush with your chosen glaze and add any topping (if using). Leave the bread to cool for at least an hour before slicing and/or removing the paddle if necessary.

- *wheat-free*
- *high-fibre*
- *gluten-free*
- *healthy heart*

SUNFLOWER SEED AND WHEATGERM BREAD

The health benefits of sunflower seeds and wheatgerm are well documented and they are combined here in a really delicious bread. Sunflower seeds are one of the cheapest sources of natural vitamin E, which is an effective antioxidant essential for healthy skin. Vitamin E is also present in wheatgerm together with folate, making this bread a useful addition to the diet of women trying to conceive and during the first 12 weeks of pregnancy.

250 ml/9 fl oz/1⅛ cups water

2 tbsp sunflower oil

2 tbsp runny honey

1 tbsp molasses

1 tsp salt

50 g/2 oz/⅝ cup wheatgerm

70 g/2½ oz/½ cup strong wholemeal flour

375 g/13 oz/2½ cups very strong white bread flour

50 g/2 oz/⅜ cup sunflower seeds

1¼ tsp instant or fast-acting dried yeast

glaze/topping (optional, see pages 162–3)

Pour the water into the breadmaker bucket and add the oil, honey and molasses. Cover the wet ingredients with the salt, wheatgerm, flours and seeds. Finally, sprinkle the yeast over. Fit the bucket into the breadmaker and set to the normal/basic white programme. Once cooked, carefully shake the loaf from the bucket and stand the right way up on a wire cooling rack. Brush with your chosen glaze and add any topping (if using). Leave the bread to cool for at least an hour before cutting and/or removing the paddle if necessary.

- egg-free
- high-fibre
- healthy heart
- low-salt
- menopause management

RAISIN SEED CAKE

The influence for this recipe came from my good friend Debbie in Cornwall, who gave me a tried and tested recipe for a PMT and menopause cake. A few additions and tweaks to the quantities resulted in this excellent cake that's perfect for snacking on throughout the day and contains ingredients helpful to so many conditions.

400 ml/14 fl oz/1⁷/₈ cups soya milk

1 tbsp malt extract

150 g/5¼ oz/1 cup raisins

50 g/2 oz/¹/₃ cup slivered almonds

25 g/1 oz/¹/₈ cup pumpkin seeds

25 g/1 oz/¹/₈ cup sunflower seeds

25 g/1 oz/¹/₈ cup sesame seeds

25 g/1 oz/¹/₈ cup linseed

75 g/3 oz/³/₄ cup rolled oats

½ tsp grated nutmeg

½ tsp ground cinnamon

½ tsp ground ginger

2 tsp grated fresh ginger

100 g/3½ oz/³/₄ cup plain wholemeal flour

100 g/3½ oz/³/₄ cup soya flour

2½ tsp baking powder

Pour the soya milk into the breadmaker bucket and add the malt extract. Add the raisins, nuts, seeds and oats. Sprinkle the dry spices and fresh ginger over. Cover with the flours and the baking powder. Fit the bucket into the machine and set to the cake programme. Lift the lid of the machine as the dough is mixing and scrape down the sides of the bucket with a plastic spatula to ensure all the ingredients are incorporated into the mix. Once cooked, carefully shake the cake from the bucket and stand the right way up on a wire cooling rack. Leave to cool for at least an hour before cutting and/or removing the paddle if necessary.

- egg-free
- low-salt
- high-fibre
- healthy heart
- yeast-free
- menopause management
- high-calcium
- diabetes management

GLUTEN-FREE RAISIN SEED CAKE

Get all the benefit of this delicious cake but without the gluten.

Follow the recipe for Raisin Seed Cake (above), but replace the rolled oats with 75 g/3 oz/³/₄ cup rice flakes and the wholemeal and soya flours with 225 g/8 oz/1½ cups gluten-free flour. As always with gluten-free recipes, ensure that all other ingredients are from a gluten-free source.

RED GRAPE AND LINSEED LOAF

This tasty bread uses only the natural sweetness of the grape juice to feed the yeast, making it a useful option if you're trying to cut down on sugar. This loaf is charmingly rugged and has a close, but fine texture. I love it simply buttered.

The compound resveratrol in red wine that is famous for being beneficial to the arteries is also found in red grape juice, giving this loaf the same healthy heart properties. Grapes also contain ellagic acid, a powerful antioxidant said to help fight cancer, and boron which is useful in preventing osteoporosis and in alleviating menopausal symptoms.

250 ml/9 fl oz/1⅛ cups unsweetened pure red grape juice

2 tbsp sunflower oil

1½ tsp salt

450 g/16 oz/3 cups very strong white bread flour

50 g/2 oz/¼ cup linseed

1½ tsp instant or fast-acting dried yeast

75 g/3 oz/½ cup raisins

glaze/topping (optional, see pages 162–3)

Pour the grape juice and sunflower oil into the breadmaker bucket and sprinkle the salt over. Cover with the flour and linseed. Sprinkle the yeast over. Fit the bucket into the breadmaker and set to the normal/basic white programme. Add the raisins according to your manual's instructions, usually at the beginning or middle of the second kneading cycle or when the machine bleeps. Once cooked, carefully shake the loaf from the bucket and stand the right way up on a wire cooling rack. Brush with your chosen glaze and add any topping (if using). Leave the bread to cool for at least an hour before cutting and/or removing the paddle if necessary.

- *dairy-free*
- *sugar-free*
- *high-fibre*
- *egg-free*
- *healthy heart*
- *menopause management*

SONIA'S HUMMUS BREAD

It's a pleasure to include Sonia's recipe for hummus bread – a light and moist loaf that is mildly savoury and speckled with chickpeas. Her recommendation is to serve it with grilled or roast chicken, grilled fish, kebabs and vegetarian dishes.

Chickpeas are an excellent food, a good source of vegetable protein, calcium, magnesium, zinc and folic acid. What's more, they are high in soluble fibre which helps cut down cholesterol levels; and, as they contain phytoestrogens, chickpeas can also help moderate the effects of oestrogen in the body thus protecting against breast cancer and menopausal symptoms.

300 ml/11 fl oz/1⅜ cups water, minus 1 tbsp

4 tsp toasted sesame oil

1 tbsp lemon juice

3 tbsp tahini (ground sesame seed paste)

1 clove of garlic, peeled and crushed (optional)

1½ tsp salt

2 tsp sugar

75 g/3 oz/6 tbsp canned cooked chickpeas, well drained

450 g/16 oz/3 cups strong white bread flour

1½ tsp instant or fast-acting dried yeast

glaze/topping (optional, see pages 162–3)

Pour the water, oil and lemon juice into the breadmaker bucket, followed by the tahini, garlic, salt and sugar. Add the chickpeas, cover with the flour and sprinkle the yeast over. Fit the bucket into the breadmaker and set to the normal/basic white programme. Once cooked, carefully shake the loaf from the bucket and stand the right way up on a wire cooling rack. Brush with your chosen glaze and add any topping (if using). Leave the bread to cool for at least an hour before cutting and/or removing the paddle if necessary.

- *dairy-free*
- *egg-free*
- *high-protein*
- *high-fibre*
- *healthy heart*
- *menopause management*

WHEAT-FREE HUMMUS BREAD

This is my variation of Sonia's original recipe, giving a delicious alternative for those trying to avoid wheat.

Follow the recipe for Hummus Bread (above), replacing the white bread flour with spelt flour and increasing the quantity of yeast to 2¼ tsp.

SWEET POTATO LOAF WITH PEPPER AND SPICE

This lovely loaf is perfect for a host of occasions from an accompaniment to barbecued meats to serving with cheese and chutney. Whatever you choose, eat it with the reassurance that it's an excellent choice for those following a healthy heart diet.

While sweet potato is a starchy carbohydrate and excellent for long-lasting energy, it is also rich in betacarotene. In fact two sweet potatoes will provide the recommended vitamin A for the average adult. In addition to this, betacarotene is a powerful antioxidant helping to neutralise the free radicals that roam the body causing heart disease, blocked arteries and even cancer.

50 ml/2 fl oz/¼ cup orange juice

50 ml/2 fl oz/¼ cup soya milk

2 tbsp canola oil

2 tbsp honey

1 tsp salt

200 g/7 oz/1 cup mashed sweet potato

50 g/2 oz/³/₈ cup sunflower seeds

½ tsp ground nutmeg

½ tsp finely ground black pepper

½ tsp ground ginger

50 g/2 oz/⁵/₈ cup wheatgerm

375 g/13 oz/2½ cups strong white bread flour

1¼ tsp instant or fast-acting dried yeast

glaze/topping (optional, see pages 162–3)

Pour the orange juice and soya milk into the breadmaker bucket, followed by the oil, honey and salt. Add the potato, seeds and spices and cover with the wheatgerm, then the flour. Finally, sprinkle the yeast over. Fit the bucket into the breadmaker and set to the normal/basic white programme. When cooked, carefully shake the loaf from the bucket and stand the right way up on a wire cooling rack. Brush with your chosen glaze and add any topping (if using). Leave to cool for at least an hour before slicing and/or removing the paddle.

- *dairy-free*
- *high-fibre*
- *healthy heart*
- *egg-free*
- *menopause management*

QUINOA AND PEANUT BUTTER BREAD

What better protein-rich bread option is there for children? Here the protein and calcium of quinoa is cleverly masked by the full flavour of peanut butter, giving a bread that the whole family will love.

In addition to their taste, peanuts are useful ingredients in helping to keep blood fats down. What's more, Chinese medicine takes full advantage of the oestrogenic compounds in peanuts, using them to help nursing mothers produce a good supply of milk.

275 ml/10 fl oz/1¼ cups water

4 tbsp crunchy peanut butter

1 tsp sugar

50 g/2 oz/½ cup quinoa flakes

70 g/2½ oz/½ cup quinoa flour

375 g/13 oz/2½ cups very strong white bread flour

1¼ tsp instant or fast-acting dried yeast

glaze/topping (optional, see pages 162–3)

Pour the water into the breadmaker bucket and add the peanut butter, sugar and quinoa flakes. Cover with the flours and sprinkle the yeast over. Fit the bucket into the breadmaker and set to the basic white programme. When cooked, carefully shake the loaf from the bucket and stand the right way up on a wire cooling rack. Brush with your chosen glaze and add any topping (if using). Leave to cool for at least an hour before slicing and/or removing the paddle.

- *egg-free*
- *high-calcium*
- *high-protein*

WHEATGERM AND APPLE BREAD WITH BRAN

This bread contains no added sugar or oil, making it an excellent choice for people with diabetes, and the addition of bran means that it's also a great source of fibre. These properties, together with providing a good source of carbohydrate, also fit the diet recommended to aid insomnia. This is because carbohydrates stimulate our bodies to produce serotonin, a sleep-inducing hormone. Served with a glass of milk, which contains the sleep-promoting amino acid tryptophan, the combination could help with sleepless nights.

250 ml/9 fl oz/1⅛ cups water

1 unpeeled eating apple, cored and grated

3 tbsp frozen concentrated orange juice, thawed and at room temperature

1 tsp salt

3 tbsp wheatgerm

3 tbsp bran

300 g/11 oz/2 cups strong brown bread flour

150 g/5¼ oz/1 cup very strong white bread flour

1½ tsp instant or fast-acting dried yeast

glaze/topping (optional, see pages 162–3)

Pour the water into the breadmaker bucket, followed by the apple, orange juice and salt. Add the wheatgerm, bran and both flours and sprinkle the yeast over. Fit the bucket into the breadmaker and set to the basic white programme. Once cooked, carefully shake the loaf from the bucket and stand the right way up on a wire cooling rack. Brush with your chosen glaze and add any topping (if using). Leave the bread to cool for at least an hour before cutting and/or removing the paddle if necessary.

- *dairy-free*
- *egg-free*
- *sugar-free*
- *high-fibre*
- *low-fat*

OATMEAL AND CRANBERRY LOAF

This wonderful bread, built on the goodness of oatmeal and wholemeal flour, is enhanced with the succulence of cranberries in every bite. Whether you enjoy it because you're a diabetic or an insomniac, you'll also benefit from the natural antibiotic and diuretic properties of cranberry and the cholesterol-reducing effect of oats. High in fibre and with no added sugar or fat, it's a great healthy all-rounder.

250 ml/9 fl oz/1⅛ cups water

3 tbsp frozen concentrated orange juice, thawed and at room temperature

1 tsp salt

75 g/3 oz/½ cup fine oatmeal

70 g/2½ oz/½ cup strong wholemeal flour

300 g/11 oz/2 cups very strong white bread flour

1½ tsp instant or fast-acting dried yeast

75 g/3 oz/½ cup ready-to-eat (semi-dried) cranberries

glaze/topping (optional, see pages 162–3)

Pour the water into the breadmaker bucket, followed by the orange juice, salt and oatmeal. Cover with the flours and sprinkle the yeast over. Fit the bucket into the breadmaker and set to the basic white programme. Add the cranberries according to your manual's instructions, usually at the beginning or middle of the second kneading cycle or when the machine bleeps. When cooked, carefully shake the loaf from the bucket and stand the right way up on a wire cooling rack. Brush with your chosen glaze and add any topping (if using). Leave to cool for at least an hour before slicing and/or removing the paddle if necessary.

- *dairy-free*
- *sugar-free*
- *low-fat*
- *healthy heart*
- *egg-free*
- *high-fibre*
- *diabetes management*

BOSTON BROWN BREAD

Traditionally Boston Brown Bread is baked in a can and served with home-made baked beans.

450 ml/16 fl oz/2 cups semi-skimmed milk

160 ml/5½ fl oz/½ cup molasses

1¼ tsp salt

150 g/5¼ oz/1 cup dried blueberries or raisins

100 g/3½ oz/½ cup polenta

150 g/5¼ oz/1 cup plain flour

150 g/5¼ oz/1 cup rye flour

150 g/5¼ oz/1 cup plain wholemeal flour

1½ tsp baking powder

1 tbsp bicarbonate of soda

Pour the milk and molasses into the breadmaker bucket. Add the salt and the dried blueberries or raisins. Sprinkle on the polenta and the flours, followed by the baking powder and bicarbonate of soda. Fit the bucket into the breadmaker and set to the cake programme. Lift the lid of the machine as the dough is mixing and scrape down the sides of the bucket with a plastic spatula to ensure all the ingredients are incorporated into the dough. Once cooked, carefully shake the loaf from the bucket and stand the right way up on a wire cooling rack. Leave to cool for at least an hour before cutting and/or removing the paddle if necessary.

- *egg-free*
- *high-fibre*
- *yeast-free*
- *low-fat*

BANANA AND CARDAMOM CAKE

This moist and spicy little cake is packed full of the goodness of bananas.

½ tsp ground cardamom seeds

¼ tsp salt

¾ tsp bicarbonate of soda

1 tsp baking powder

190 g/6½ oz/1¼ cups plain flour

50 ml/2 fl oz/¼ cup water

2 ripe bananas, mashed

2 eggs, beaten

4 tbsp runny honey

Put the cardamom, salt, bicarbonate of soda, baking powder and flour into a bowl and mix together thoroughly. Pour the water into the breadmaker bucket, followed by the bananas, eggs and honey. Cover with the flour mixture. Fit the bucket into the breadmaker and set to the cake programme. Once cooked, carefully shake the cake from the bucket and stand the right way up on a wire cooling rack. Leave to cool for at least an hour before cutting and/or removing the paddle if necessary.

- *dairy-free*
- *yeast-free*
- *high-fibre*
- *sugar-free*
- *low-salt*
- *low-fat*

DATE, APPLE AND WALNUT LOAF

This yeast- and gluten-free loaf is high in fibre. The pectin from the apple eases bowel disorders and walnuts have been used for centuries in Turkey to treat glandular problems including thyroid imbalances.

225 g/8 oz/1½ cups rice flour

1½ tsp gluten-free baking powder

¾ tsp bicarbonate of soda

½ tsp xanthum gum

½ tsp salt

4 tbsp light soft brown sugar

4 tbsp melted butter

3 medium eggs, beaten

125 ml/4 fl oz/½ cup water

1 unpeeled eating apple, cored and grated

50 g/2 oz/½ cup chopped walnuts

75 g/3 oz/⅝ cup chopped dates

In a bowl mix together the flour, baking powder, bicarbonate of soda, gum, salt and sugar. Pour the melted butter, eggs and water into the breadmaker bucket, followed by the apple, nuts and dates. Pour the flour mixture over the top. Fit the bucket into the breadmaker and set to the cake programme. When cooked, carefully shake the loaf from the bucket and stand the right way up on a wire cooling rack. Leave to cool.

- *wheat-free*
- *yeast-free*
- *gluten-free*
- *high-fibre*

TOMATO BREAD WITH QUINOA AND SPINACH

No health chapter would be complete without a mention of Popeye's favourite – spinach. And what better partner than the protein-rich quinoa? In this distinctive loaf, both combine with tomato to produce a rich orange bread, with a wonderful crust that's speckled throughout with fresh green spinach.

The health claims for spinach are far reaching: it has been associated with treating chronic fatigue (ME); it is linked to helping prevent heart disease and strokes; it is a rich source of folate for pregnant women; and it is also high in zinc, a mineral essential for maintaining male fertility. Maybe that's where Popeye comes in!

300 ml/11 fl oz/1³/₈ cups water

2 tbsp tomato purée

1 tbsp sunflower oil

¹/₄ tsp ground nutmeg

2 tsp sugar

1¹/₂ tsp salt

30 small fresh spinach leaves, stalks removed

3 tbsp wheatgerm

70 g/2¹/₂ oz/¹/₂ cup quinoa flour

375 g/13 oz/2¹/₂ cups very strong white bread flour

1¹/₄ tsp instant or fast-acting dried yeast

glaze/topping (optional, see pages 162–3)

Pour the water into the breadmaker bucket, followed by the tomato purée and oil. Add the nutmeg, sugar and salt and then the spinach leaves. Cover with the wheatgerm and flours and sprinkle the yeast over. Fit the bucket into the breadmaker and set to the basic white programme. When cooked, carefully shake the loaf from the bucket and stand the right way up on a wire cooling rack. Brush with your chosen glaze and add any topping (if using). Leave to cool for at least an hour before slicing and/or removing the paddle.

- *egg-free*
- *high-calcium*
- *high-protein*
- *dairy-free*

Delicious Doughs
and Finishing Touches

Doughs

If you've never made dough in your breadmaker then you're in for a surprise. Forget all that laborious mixing and kneading – the machine will do all this for you and the result is a beautifully smooth, airy dough ready for you to shape, prove and bake in the traditional way.

But why would you want to make dough when the machine makes such fabulous bread, I hear you ask? Well, think of pizza, beautiful round flat breads brushed with olive oil, and muffins. All of these can be made with ease using the dough cycle plus a little extra time from you to shape the dough and then to bake it in the conventional way. You'll be amazed at how easy it is to make bread specialities in this way; with the hard work done for you, you'll have maximum time and enthusiasm to let your imagination run wild.

The other great thing I've found about the dough cycle is that fresh bread dough is a great way to amuse children. It can take no end of bashing, rolling and pulling by a child and still produce something edible. And, what better way to get children baking than with such a popular dish as pizza?

Helpful Hints for Making Dough

• In some machines it may be necessary to leave the dough to rise in the bucket even after the programme has finished. Leave it until it has either doubled in size or nearly reached the top of the bucket.

• I'd always recommend leaving dough to rise slowly at room temperature. As long as it's in a draught-free position it will rise, given time. If, however, time is short you can resort to the airing cupboard. Similarly, if you want to delay the length of time until your dough is ready to bake, it can be put in the fridge then brought out and allowed to finish rising at room temperature before baking.

• For loaves and general breadmaking I find non-stick bakeware the most convenient. The exception to this is when baking pizza, when my personal preference is NOT to use non-stick, so the pizza may be cut on the tray without damaging the surface of the tin itself. If you don't have non-stick tins, using baking parchment or a Teflon baking sheet cover on regular bakeware is an excellent alternative.

• If you have a fan oven you may need to reduce the baking temperature slightly – usually by about 10–20°C depending on the recipe.

• For instructions on storing and freezing dough see page 17.

FOUGASSE

This leaf-shaped flat bread originated from the Christmas Eve celebration feast in Provence where it was shaped to symbolise Jesus and the Apostles. Today, this distinctive bread has found its way into the speciality bread sections of many supermarkets, as it's an excellent choice for informal dining and an attractive centrepiece for the table.

225 ml/8 fl oz/1 cup water

75 ml/3 fl oz/³/₈ cup olive oil, plus extra for brushing

1 tbsp sugar

2 tsp salt

450 g/16 oz/3 cups strong white bread flour

2½ tsp instant or fast-acting dried yeast

Makes 2

Pour the water and oil into the breadmaker bucket, followed by the sugar and salt. Cover with the flour and sprinkle the yeast over. Fit the bucket into the breadmaker and set to the dough programme. When the cycle is complete, turn the dough out on to a lightly floured surface and divide in half. Flatten each half with your hands or a rolling pin to form a leaf shape approximately 1.5 cm/³/₄ in thick. Put each leaf on an oiled baking sheet. To form the distinctive shape, make diagonal slashes from the centre of the dough outwards so the cuts look like the veins on a leaf. Carefully open out each of the slashes to make the slashes into oval holes, stretching the dough to its final shape. Cover with a damp tea towel and leave to prove until springy to the touch. Brush with olive oil and bake in a preheated oven at 200°C/400°F/gas mark 6 for 20–25 minutes until golden. Remove from the oven and brush again with olive oil. Transfer to a wire cooling rack and leave until cool.

FOUGASSE WITH FRAGRANT HERBS

Give your fougasse the flavour and aroma of a summer's day by adding herbs to the dough.

Follow the recipe for Fougasse (above), adding 1½ tbsp herbes de Provence with the flour.

PITTA BREAD

If you've never tried making your own pitta bread I think you'll be surprised at just how easy it is, especially as the breadmaker takes all the work out of making the dough. It's one of those recipes that children love helping to make. Pitta breads are relatively quick to prepare and are a perfect option for a midday snack. Alternatively, stuff pittas with a tasty filling for a packed lunch or picnic.

275 ml/10 fl oz/1¼ cups water

½ tsp sugar

1 tsp salt

2 tbsp olive oil

450 g/16 oz/3 cups strong white bread flour

1½ tsp instant or fast-acting dried yeast

Makes 8

Pour the water into the breadmaker bucket, followed by the sugar and salt. Add the oil, then cover all the wet ingredients with the flour. Finally, sprinkle the yeast over. Fit the bucket into the breadmaker and set to the dough programme. When the cycle is complete, turn the dough out on to a lightly floured surface and knead until smooth. Divide the dough into eight pieces and shape each piece into a ball. Using a rolling pin, roll each ball of dough into a flat oval about 5 mm/¼ in thick. Cover the pittas with a damp tea towel and leave to prove for about 15–20 minutes until slightly risen. Meanwhile, preheat the oven to 220°C/425°F/gas mark 7. Dust two baking sheets with flour and place them in the oven to preheat for 5 minutes. When the pittas are ready to cook, place them on the hot baking sheets and quickly return them to the oven. They'll take only 7–10 minutes to puff up and cook. Once baked, remove from the oven and wrap in a clean tea towel to stop them drying out.

WHOLEMEAL PITTA BREAD

Follow the recipe for Pitta Bread (above), using 375 g/13 oz/2½ cups strong white bread flour and 70 g/2½ oz/½ cup strong wholemeal flour to make the dough.

GRISSINI (BREADSTICKS)

While grissini are traditionally an accompaniment to antipasto in Italy, here they are most often served with dips. I've also found that they are an excellent low-fat snack for children, who love helping to make them. If you're going to the trouble of making your own breadsticks, don't be too fussy about achieving a beautifully even shape. Slightly irregular grissini look home-made and will be admired by your guests.

250 ml/9 fl oz/1⅛ cups water

3 tbsp olive oil

1 tsp malt extract

2 tsp salt

2 tbsp semolina, plus extra for dusting

450 g/16 oz/3 cups strong white bread flour

2½ tsp instant or fast-acting dried yeast

Egg wash (see page 163)

sea salt, sesame seeds and chopped rosemary, for topping

Makes 30–40

Pour the water and oil into the breadmaker bucket, followed by the malt extract and salt. Cover with the semolina and flour. Finally, add the yeast. Fit the bucket into the breadmaker and set to the dough programme. When the cycle is complete, turn the dough out on to a lightly floured surface and knead until smooth. Divide the dough into 30–40 pieces. Shape each piece into a round and then an oval. Continue to roll the oval running your fingers along the dough to form very thin sticks about 25 cm/10 in long. Oil the required number of baking sheets and dust them with semolina. Place the dough sticks 2.5 cm/½ in apart on the baking sheets, brush them with the egg wash and sprinkle on the toppings. Bake at 200°C/400°F/gas mark 6 for 15–20 minutes until crisp and golden. Transfer to a wire cooling rack and leave until cool.

FRENCH STICKS

Crispy on the outside with a moist, chewy centre, these rustic-style French sticks are delicious served at any meal, whether it's with preserves for breakfast, with soup for lunch, or alongside a casserole for supper.

300 ml/11 fl oz/1³/₈ cups water

1½ tsp salt

1 tsp sugar

450 g/16 oz/3 cups strong white bread flour

1½ tsp instant or fast-acting dried yeast

Makes 2 or 3

Pour the water into the breadmaker bucket, followed by the salt and sugar. Cover the liquid with the flour and sprinkle the yeast over. Fit the bucket into the breadmaker and set to the dough programme. When the cycle is complete, turn the dough out on to a floured board and divide into two or three pieces depending on the length of sticks your oven will allow. Roll each piece of dough into a long, thin stick and transfer to lightly greased baking sheets. Cover with a tea towel and leave in a warm place until doubled in size. Brush with water and bake at 220°C/425°F/gas mark 7 for 15 minutes until crisp and golden.

NOTE: for an even crisper crust you can spray the sticks with water 2 or 3 times while they are in the oven. A plant mister is an excellent tool for this task.

PRETZELS

See for yourself how quick and easy pretzels are to make with a home-made breadmaker dough.

225 ml/8 fl oz/1 cup water

1½ tsp salt

1 tsp sugar

450 g/16 oz/3 cups strong white bread flour

2½ tsp instant or fast-acting dried yeast

Egg wash (see page 163)

sea salt and sesame seeds, for topping

Makes 8–10

Pour the water into the breadmaker bucket and add the salt and sugar. Cover with the flour and sprinkle the yeast over. Fit the bucket into the breadmaker and set to the dough programme. When the cycle is complete, turn the dough out on to a lightly floured surface and knead until smooth. Divide into 8–10 equal-sized pieces. Shape each piece into a round and then an oval. Continue to roll the oval, running your fingers along the dough to make a long strip about 40 cm/16 in long with a thick piece of dough in the centre. To twist each piece of dough into the traditional pretzel shape, simply pick up each end of the strip to make a loop, then cross the dough over twice at the base of the loop and press the ends down each side of the thick centre. Repeat this action with the remaining dough pieces. Place the pretzels on an oiled baking sheet and leave to prove until doubled in size. Brush with the egg wash and sprinkle with either sea salt or sesame seeds. Bake at 200°C/400°F/gas mark 6 for 15–20 minutes until golden. Transfer to a wire rack and leave until cool.

ONION BAGELS

These home-made bagels are just like the real thing; lightly toasted and spread with cream cheese they're heavenly. If you prefer plain bagels omit the onion flakes and serve with a range of sweet or savoury toppings.

225 ml/8 fl oz/1 cup water

1½ tbsp sugar

1½ tsp salt

2 tbsp dried onion flakes

450 g/16 oz/3 cups strong white bread flour

2 tsp instant or fast-acting dried yeast

Egg wash (see page 163)

poppy seeds and sesame seeds, for topping (optional)

Makes 8

Pour the water into the breadmaker bucket and add the sugar, salt and onion flakes. Top with the flour and sprinkle the yeast over. Fit the bucket into the breadmaker and set to the dough programme. When the cycle is complete, turn the dough out on to a lightly floured surface and knead until smooth. Divide into eight equal-sized pieces. Shape each piece of dough into a ball and then use your finger to make a hole in the centre, stretching the dough out to form the traditional bagel shape. Stretch each bagel to widen the hole. Place the bagels on an oiled baking sheet, cover with a damp tea towel and leave to rest for 10 minutes. Meanwhile, bring a large pan of water to the boil and reduce the heat so the water stays at a simmer. Poach the bagels a couple at a time for about 1 minute, turning them over if they rise to the surface before the poaching time is up. Once poached, remove the bagels from the pan with a slotted spoon, drain and transfer to a second lightly oiled baking sheet. Brush with the egg wash and sprinkle with the sesame or poppy seeds (if using). Bake the bagels in a preheated oven at 220°C/425°F/gas mark 7 for 20 minutes until golden.

NAAN BREAD

You'll be amazed at how quick and easy it is to make your own naan bread.

250 ml/9 fl oz/1⅛ cups semi-skimmed milk

3 tbsp natural yoghurt

1 tsp sugar

1½ tsp salt

2 tbsp melted unsalted butter or ghee

450 g/16 oz/3 cups strong white bread flour

1¼ tsp instant or fast-acting dried yeast

Makes 4

Pour the milk into the breadmaker bucket, followed by the yoghurt, sugar, salt and butter or ghee. Cover with the flour and finally sprinkle the yeast over. Fit the bucket into the breadmaker and set to the dough programme. When the cycle is complete, turn the dough out on to a lightly floured surface and knead until smooth. Divide into four equal-sized pieces. Roll out each piece to an oval about 5 mm/¼ in thick. Preheat the grill to its highest setting and heat a baking sheet under it for a couple of minutes. Cook the naans two at a time under the grill for about 2–3 minutes on each side until puffy and golden. Once cooked, wrap the breads in a clean tea towel to prevent drying out and serve hot.

If you want to make the nans ahead of time simply re-heat in the oven, or for a few seconds in the microwave.

BLUEBERRY MUFFINS

These light and chewy muffins are studded with succulent blueberries, making them a delicious treat at any time of day. They're especially good as part of a picnic or packed lunch, or served warm for brunch. Semi-dried blueberries can be found in most supermarkets with the other ready-to-eat semi-dried fruit.

75 ml/3 fl oz/³/8 cup milk

1 large egg, beaten

150 ml/5 fl oz/⁵/8 cup water

1 tbsp sunflower oil

3 tbsp demerara sugar

1¹/2 tsp salt

225 g/8 oz/1¹/2 cups spelt flour

225 g/8 oz/1¹/2 cups strong white bread flour

2¹/2 tsp instant or fast-acting dried yeast

75 g/3 oz/¹/2 cup semi-dried blueberries

Makes 16

Pour the milk, egg, water and oil into the breadmaker bucket. Add the sugar and salt. Cover with the flours and finally sprinkle the yeast over. Fit the bucket into the breadmaker and set to the dough programme. Add the blueberries according to your manual's instructions, usually at the beginning or middle of the second kneading cycle or when the machine bleeps. When the dough cycle is complete, turn the dough out on to a lightly floured surface. Divide the dough into 16 equal-sized pieces. Roll each piece into a ball and then flatten to about 2.5 cm/1 in thick. Put the muffins on lightly greased baking sheets, cover with a tea towel and leave to prove in a warm place until doubled in size. Bake at 200°C/400°F/gas mark 6 for 10–15 minutes.

Perfect Pizza

Comfort food at its best, nothing beats the taste of a generously proportioned and fresh-from-the-oven home-made pizza: its crust amber-coloured and puffy, its texture light and crisp, its deli-style toppings appetising and meltingly fragrant. Almost all the pizzas in this section work out much tastier and less costly than anything you can buy from a shop – or indeed have to pay for from a home-delivery service – and, as you read on, you will see that the variety of toppings on offer is infinitely wider and much more personal than the predictable off-the-peg selection you get if you buy rather than make.

As a starting point, I give you a practical basic recipe that can be covered with a variety of assorted toppings to suit all family tastes and fortunes. It's made very simply from a bread machine dough, beautifully worked and smooth, and sufficient for two 30 cm/12 in pizzas – enough to serve eight people.

If two pizzas are too much for one meal, wrap and freeze the spare one for later; you'll be really glad it's there when you want to put a tasty meal on the table in minutes. If you would prefer to keep the dough for another time, wrap it up securely and freeze. When you want to use the dough, ensure that it's defrosted and brought up to room temperature before using it to make another pizza.

Bakeware

My personal preference here is for tins that are NOT non-stick, so the pizza may be cut on the tray without damaging the surface of the tin itself.

BASIC PIZZA DOUGH

The ultimate pizza dough. Try it with the following toppings, or be innovative and create your own.

275 ml/10 fl oz/1¼ cups water

2 tbsp olive oil

2 tsp salt

2 tsp sugar

450 g/16 oz/3 cups strong white bread flour

2½ tsp instant or fast-acting dried yeast

Makes 2

Pour the water into the breadmaker bucket, followed by the oil, salt and sugar. Cover with the flour and sprinkle the yeast over. Fit the bucket into the breadmaker and set to the dough progamme. When the dough cycle is complete, turn the dough out and quickly knead on a floured surface. Divide in half and roll each piece into a round large enough to cover an oiled and floured-dusted 30 cm/12 in pizza tin. Cover with toppings to within 2.5 cm/1 in of the edges then, for a thin crust, refrigerate the prepared pizza for 30 minutes before baking or, for a distinct puffy edge, leave the pizza to rise in the warmth of the kitchen for about 30 minutes. In either case it is important to cover the pizza with a piece of oiled foil to prevent it drying out. Bake in a preheated oven at 220°C/425°F/gas mark 7 for 20–25 minutes.

TOPPINGS

All the toppings given are for one pizza only. Follow the Basic Pizza Dough instructions (opposite), covering the dough base to within 2.5 cm/1 in of the edges.

PIZZA NAPOLETANA

A classic from Naples, served in pizzeria since the end of the 19th century.

4 tbsp tomato purée

200 g/7 oz thinly sliced or coarsely grated Mozzarella cheese

1 tbsp chopped fresh oregano or 1–1½ tsp dried

1 x 50 g/2 oz can of anchovies in oil (sprinkle the oil on top of the pizza)

PIZZA PEPERONI

A Chicago-style topping that makes for a familiar and tasty pizza.

4 tbsp tomato purée

200 g/7 oz thinly sliced or coarsely grated Mozarella cheese

1 tbsp chopped fresh oregano or 1–1½ tsp dried

50 g/2 oz very thinly sliced peperoni sausage

1 large green pepper, cut into strips and simmered for 3–4 minutes in boiling water, then thoroughly drained

4 tbsp grated Parmesan cheese

PIZZA MARINARA

The simplest of its kind, and totally vegetarian too, this is popular 'hawker food' in Naples.

5 tbsp passata

4 medium tomatoes, thinly sliced

2–3 peeled and crushed garlic cloves mixed with

3 tbsp olive oil

1 tbsp chopped fresh oregano or 1–1½ tsp dried

PIZZA MARGHERITA

In this pizza the tomatoes, cheese and basil are said to represent the colours of the Italian flag.

4 tbsp tomato purée

4 medium tomatoes, thinly sliced

200 g/7 oz thinly sliced or coarsely grated Mozzarella cheese

12 torn-up fresh basil leaves or 1½ tsp dried

4 tbsp grated Parmesan cheese

Pizza Plus Selection

Here's some additional inspiration for truly distinctive home-made pizza. The recipes combine flavourings in the dough itself as well as some more unusual toppings.

PIZZA SCOTS STYLE

Keep this one for entertaining! The marriage of flavours is unique and sophisticated, the whisky blending exquisitely with the fish, the cheese and the toasted oats. The salmon and the oats need a little pre-preparation, so remember to allow time for this.

FOR THE DOUGH

5 tbsp lightly toasted oats

300 ml/11 fl oz/1³/₈ cups water

2 tbsp corn, grapeseed or sunflower oil

2 tsp salt

2 tsp sugar

450 g/16 oz/3 cups strong white bread flour

2¹/₂ tsp instant or fast-acting dried yeast

FOR THE TOPPING

100 g/3¹/₂ oz smoked salmon, cut into strips

125 g/4 oz poached fresh salmon

3 tbsp whisky

4 tbsp tomato purée

200 g/7 oz/2 cups grated Cheddar cheese, Scottish for preference

¹/₂ teacupful small parsley springs

Makes 2

Place the smoked and fresh salmon in a non-metallic bowl and pour the whisky over. Leave to marinate for 3 hours. Toss the oats in a dry frying pan for a few seconds until lightly toasted, then set aside.

To make the dough, pour the water into the breadmaker bucket, followed by the oil, salt and sugar. Cover with the flour, the toasted oats and finally sprinkle the yeast over. Fit the bucket into the breadmaker and set to the dough programme. When the cycle is complete, turn the dough out and quickly knead on a floured surface. Divide in half and roll each piece into a round large enough to cover an oiled and flour-dusted 30 cm/12 in pizza tin, gently pulling and stretching the dough until it reaches the edges of the tin.

To assemble the pizza, cover to within 2.5 cm/1 in of the edges with the tomato purée, followed by the marinated salmon and the whisky. Sprinkle with the cheese and top with parsley sprigs. For a thin crust, refrigerate the prepared pizza for 30 minutes before baking or, for a distinct puffy edge, leave the pizza to rise in the warmth of the kitchen, also for about 30 minutes. In either case it is important to cover the pizza with a piece of oiled foil to prevent it drying out. Bake the pizza for 20–25 minutes in a preheated oven at 220°C/425°F/ gas mark 7.

SUNDRIED RED PEPPER AND PESTO PIZZA WITH BRESOLA

An atmospheric pizza with a punch to it, made for icy cold lager or foaming glasses of Guinness. The Bresola sweet-cured beef comes from the Lombardy region of Italy.

FOR THE DOUGH

300 ml/11 fl oz/1³/₈ cups water

1 tbsp olive oil

2 tbsp pesto

1 tsp salt

2 tsp sugar

450 g/16 oz/3 cups strong white bread flour

2¹/₂ tsp instant or fast-acting dried yeast

FOR THE TOPPING

4 tbsp tomato purée

25 g/1 oz sundried red peppers, torn into strips

80 g/just over 3 oz Bresola

250 g/8 oz Mozarella cheese, thinly sliced

12 fresh basil leaves

To make the dough, pour the water into the breadmaker bucket, followed by the oil, pesto, salt and sugar. Cover with the flour and sprinkle the yeast over. Fit the bucket into the breadmaker and set to the dough programme. When the cycle is complete, turn the dough out and quickly knead on a floured surface. Divide in half and roll each piece into a round large enough to cover an oiled and flour-dusted 30 cm/12 in pizza tin, gently pulling and stretching the dough until it reaches the edges of the tin.

To assemble the pizza, cover to within 2.5 cm/1 in of the edges with the tomato purée, followed by the sundried tomato strips and Bresola. Lay the cheese slices on top and dot here and there with the basil leaves. For a thin crust, refrigerate the prepared pizza for 30 minutes before baking or, for a distinct puffy edge, leave the pizza to rise in the warmth of the kitchen, also for about 30 minutes. In either case it is important to cover the pizza with a piece of oiled foil to prevent it drying out. Bake the pizza for 20–25 minutes in a preheated oven at 220°C/425°F/gas mark 7.

TUNA AND CAPER PIZZA WITH FRESH LIME AND SUNDRIED TOMATO OIL

Abundant with canned tuna and scented with lime, this pizza has shades of East and West and makes a fabulous and fulfilling meal with a glass of chilled Muscadet or Gewürztraminer.

FOR THE DOUGH

275 ml/10 fl oz/1¼ cups water

3 tbsp Italian sundried tomato-infused extra virgin olive oil

2 tsp salt

2 tsp sugar

grated zest of 1 lime

2 tsp chopped fresh mint or ½ tsp dried

450 g/16 oz/3 cups strong white bread flour

2½ tsp instant or fast-acting dried yeast

FOR THE TOPPING

4 tbsp sundried tomato paste

2 medium cans of tuna in olive oil

6 tsp capers

6 tbsp grated Parmesan cheese

To make the dough, pour the water into the breadmaker bucket, followed by the oil, salt, sugar, lime and mint. Cover with the flour and sprinkle the yeast over. Fit the bucket into the breadmaker and set to the dough programme. When the cycle is complete, turn the dough out and quickly knead on a floured surface. Divide in half and roll each piece into a round large enough to cover an oiled and flour-dusted 30 cm/12 in pizza tin, gently pulling and stretching the dough until it reaches the edges of the tin.

To assemble the pizza, cover to within 2.5 cm/1 in of the edges with the tomato paste. Flake up the tuna and half of its oil and spread over the tomato. Sprinkle with the capers and the Parmesan. For a thin crust, refrigerate the prepared pizza for 30 minutes before baking or, for a distinct puffy edge, leave the pizza to rise in the warmth of the kitchen, also for about 30 minutes. In either case it is important to cover the pizza with a piece of oiled foil to prevent it drying out. Bake the pizza for 20–25 minutes in a preheated oven at 220°C/425°F/gas mark 7.

FINISHING TOUCHES

As with all things culinary, it's the finishing touches that turn a good dish into something really special, so it's worth taking time to read through the sections below to see how you can make your home-made bread extra special.

DOUGH SHAPES AND ROLLS

Basic dough made in the breadmaker can be used as the base for virtually any shape of roll or loaf. Let your imagination run wild. Try cottage loaves, plaits, twists or even using wholemeal and white dough twisted together to make a single multi-textured loaf.

DOUGH BALLS

One of my favourite ways to use dough is to make dough balls. I like to serve them piled high on a platter with melted Garlic and Herb Butter for dipping. Smaller marble-sized dough balls take only a few minutes to bake and make an attractive alternative to croutons when sprinkled on a bowl of salad.

1 quantity of Basic Pizza Dough (see page 154)

Olive oil, for brushing

Garlic and Herb Butter, to serve (see page 164)

Makes 50–60

Follow the instruction for Basic Pizza Dough. When the dough cycle is complete, turn the dough out on to a lightly floured surface and knead until smooth. Take walnut-sized pieces from the dough and roll into balls. Place the balls on oiled baking sheets, cover with a tea towel and leave to prove until doubled in size. Brush with olive oil and bake for 10–15 minutes at 220°C/425°F/gas mark 7.

CROSTINI (CROUTES)

These versatile slices of crisp bread are the perfect base for canapés. I like to make them with a day-old French loaf.

Cut the bread into 1 cm/1/2 in slices and place on a baking sheet. Bake in a preheated oven at 180°C/350°F/gas mark 4 for approximately 10–15 minutes until crisp.

CROUTONS

Serve with soup or salad.

Cut 1 cm/1/2 in slices from a loaf of your choice. Trim off the crusts and cut the bread into 1 cm/1/2 in cubes (or use a small cutter to make other shapes if you prefer). Heat some butter and oil in a frying pan over a low heat until hot enough to sizzle when one of the cubes is put in. Add the cubes to the pan in a single layer and fry until crisp, turning them over to give an even colour. Remove the crisp croutons from the pan and drain on kitchen paper. Leave to cool.

TOPPINGS AND GLAZES

Adding toppings and glazes is undoubtedly the quickest and easiest way to make your rolls and loaves look really special. Creating a beautiful shiny crust or adding a crunchy topping of seeds and nuts or even a brush of your favourite beer can all make a difference to the finished loaf.

When making dough-based recipes adding toppings and glazes is easy: simply brush the proved dough with your chosen glaze and bake. Alternatively, for high-sugar glazes apply the glaze once the bread has been removed from the oven. Toppings are best applied after a glaze, as the glaze will help them adhere to the bread.

When baking in the breadmaker it's not so obvious when to apply a glaze or topping. The easiest way, as directed in most of the recipes in this book, is to brush the chosen glaze on to the hot loaf after removing it from the bucket at the end of the cycle. However, because of concerns many of us have about eating only fully cooked eggs, I do lift the lid during the cycle when applying an egg-based glaze. In this way you can be sure that the glaze will bake along with the bread during the final stage of the cycle.

If your machine's manual gives a breakdown of programme stages you'll be able to see how long your baking cycle is and apply egg and toppings at the appropriate time. If you don't have this information, as a rough guide most machines are baking during the last 45 minutes of the cycle. Take care lifting the lid when the machine is operating – it will be HOT and steam often puffs out. Have everything ready and your glaze at room temperature. To apply, simply lift the lid, brush on the glaze followed by any topping (if using) and close the lid again.

Like most breadmaker techniques, it's about finding out what works best for you and you'll be able to decide on this by using the information in this chapter and the instructions in your machine's manual.

TOPPINGS

Toppings will add even more variety to your loaves and are best added immediately after a glaze. Try some of the ideas below.

SEEDS

There is a wide choice of seeds and seed blends available from health food stores and supermarkets – use them on both sweet and savoury breads. Whether you choose sunflower, poppy, pumpkin, sesame or caraway or a mixture, they're best applied after a glaze of Egg Wash (see page 163).

GRAINS

Take a few minutes looking in the health food shop at the wide selection of whole and cracked grains that can make wholesome, rustic toppings for savoury breads.

BRAN

Bran flakes will improve the fibre content and make a wonderfully textured topping.

OATS

Choose from a wide range of grades and textures from rolled oats to oatmeal.

FLOUR

For a soft, dusty finish sift flour over the shaped dough before proving and again before baking. Try experimenting with the more unusual speciality flours mentioned earlier in this book (see pages 13–17).

POLENTA

Apply a sprinkling of polenta or cornmeal over proved dough brushed with a little water to give a crisp, golden topping.

SUGAR

For sweet breads glaze with Egg Wash (see page 163) and sprinkle with sugar.

SALT

Add a continental touch by finishing savoury flat breads with a sprinkling of sea salt.

CHEESE

Cheese is one of the most popular toppings, but is also potentially one of the messiest. I think it's best applied to the finished hot bread and allowed to melt gently. Alternatively you could add it 5 minutes before the end of the cycle. Parmesan is particularly good applied before baking over an Egg Wash (see page 163) or water.

HERBS

Don't restrict yourself to dried herbs – use fresh herbs too. Whether sprinkled on flat breads, rolls or loaves, fresh herbs will produce a lovely finish and add both flavour and texture to the finished bread.

GLAZES

Glazes will add interest to your bread by providing a variety of finishes to the crust. Some glazes add flavour and some also vary the texture of the crust. Experiment with some of the ideas below.

EGG WASH

Whisk together 1 egg, 1 tbsp water and a pinch of salt. Brush over proved dough just before baking for a shiny, golden crust.

MILK

Milk will also give a golden crust. For sweet bread recipes a little sugar can also be added to warm milk and then brushed on the dough.

WATER

For a French-style finish, brush your loaf with warm water at the beginning of the baking cycle. To increase the effect, you can brush or spray (see page 148) the loaf up to three times during baking, but make sure the crust is dry each time otherwise it may go soggy. Also take care when adding water; if it drips on to the hot bucket or the element it will produce steam!

SALT WATER

To give a shiny surface and a crisp crust, brush your bread with lightly salted water immediately before the baking cycle.

SOYA POWDER AND WATER

Excellent for vegans and a superb egg-free alternative to egg wash. Mix soya powder with water and brush on proved dough just before the baking cycle.

CORNFLOUR AND WATER

Simply mix a little cornflour with some water and cook over a low heat until translucent. Allow to cool slightly and apply to dough before baking to give a shiny, chewy crust.

BEER

For a rich and shiny crust use your favourite beer, but make sure it's at room temperature as beer straight from the fridge could cause the dough to collapse.

OLIVE OIL

Brushing with olive oil immediately before and again after baking will give a subtle flavour and a rich, shiny crust. I love this on focaccia and traditional flatbreads.

BUTTER

Melt a little butter or margarine in the microwave or over a low heat and brush over the crust of a cooked loaf (while still hot) to produce a richly flavoured crust with a softer texture.

JAM, HONEY AND SYRUP

Sweet glazes are best applied directly on to the crust of hot baked bread. Try melted apricot jam flavoured with a sprinkle of cinnamon, or runny honey, maple syrup, golden syrup or even molasses.

FLAVOURED BUTTERS

There's no better accompaniment to real home-made bread than butter, and no bread bible would be complete without some recipes for delicious flavoured butters. Here are some of my favourites.

To make a flavoured butter, simply cream the softened butter until smooth, beat in the additional ingredients, then chill until required. For spreading, allow the butter to come to room temperature before use. For an alternative presentation, form the flavoured butter into a roll and wrap in greaseproof paper. Chill until required and serve in individual slices.

GARLIC AND HERB BUTTER
50 g/2 oz butter, softened

1 large clove of garlic, crushed

2 tsp chopped fresh parsley

1 tbsp lemon juice

salt and freshly ground black pepper

MUSTARD AND MINT BUTTER
50 g/2 oz butter, softened

1/2 tsp Dijon mustard, or to taste

1 tbsp fresh chopped mint

salt and freshly ground black pepper

LEMON AND HERB BUTTER
50 g/2 oz butter, softened

grated rind of 1 lemon

2 tsp lemon juice

1 tsp finely chopped fresh parsley

salt and freshly ground black pepper

CINNAMON BUTTER
50 g/2 oz butter, softened

1 tbsp icing sugar

1 tbsp ground cinnamon

CHOC AND NUT BUTTER
50 g/2 oz butter, softened

1 tsp caster sugar

1/2 tbsp finely grated chocolate

1 tbsp very finely chopped nuts, e.g. hazelnuts or walnuts

LEMON BUTTER
50 g/2 oz butter, softened

1 tbsp icing sugar

grated rind of 1 lemon

1 tbsp lemon juice

ORANGE BUTTER
50 g/2 oz butter, softened

1 tbsp icing sugar

grated rind of 1 orange

1 tbsp orange juice

Common Problems

If you're not entirely satisfied with your loaf, use the following troubleshooting guide to help you. Dough problems (e.g. too wet or too dry) can be corrected during the cycle. See also the important measuring notes on page 169.

The dough is crumbly and does not form a soft ball

There is insufficient liquid in the dough. Add more liquid 1 tbsp at a time during the kneading cycle until a soft dough is formed.

The dough is very sticky and does not form a ball

The dough is too wet. Add a little flour, 1 tbsp at a time, waiting for it to be fully integrated before adding more.

The dough has not mixed or only partially mixed

Either you forgot to fit the paddle into the bucket or the paddle was not fixed properly into the shaft. Alternatively, the bucket was not correctly fitted into the machine.

The bread has mixed but not baked

The dough cycle was selected. Either remove the dough from the bucket and bake in the oven, or use the bake cycle of the machine.

There is a smell of burning and smoke is coming from the machine

Ingredients or dough have been spilled on the heating element. Wipe the machine out with a damp cloth once it is cold.

The bread rose too much

This could be due to the following reasons:
- There is too much yeast in the recipe; try reducing the yeast by 1/4 tsp next time.
- There is too much sugar or other sweet ingredients in the recipe.
- You have forgotten to add salt to the dough.
- The recipe contained too much dough volume for the capacity of your machine. Check your manufacturer's handbook to ensure that the quantities in the recipe did not exceed the maximum amount of flour recommended for your breadmaker.

The bread did not rise enough

There are a number of possible reasons for this:
- There is not enough yeast in the dough. Or, the yeast may be inactive because it is out of date or it was killed off because the liquid was too hot when you added it to the bucket.
- The yeast and salt came into contact with each other prior to the dough mixing.
- If you chose a rapid cycle, the bread may not have had sufficient time to rise.
- No sugar or other sweet ingredients were added. Yeast needs some sugar to feed it (however, too much will retard the yeast).
- There was too much salt in the recipe. You may have used a tbsp measure rather than a tsp, or added the salt twice.

• You used an unsuitable flour. Remember, bread made with heavier flours like wholemeal and rye will not rise as high as their white equivalents and must be mixed with strong white bread flour to produce satisfactory loaves in a breadmaker. Gluten-free loaves will also not rise as high and will generally have a more cakey texture than traditional bread (see page 15).

• The dough was too dry to rise properly. Add more water next time or, if you notice the dough is dry during the programme, add 1/2 tbsp water during the kneading cycle until the dough is soft and pliable.

The bread did not rise at all

No yeast was added, or the yeast added was inactive because it had been killed off by other ingredients, or from being too hot, or was past its sell-by date.

The bread collapsed after rising or during baking

There are a number of factors that can produce this result:

• The dough was too wet. Either reduce the liquid by 1/2 tbsp next time or add a little more flour.

• There was too much yeast in the mixture. Reduce the amount of yeast slightly next time.

• Not enough salt was added to control the action of the yeast.

• High humidity or warm weather can cause the dough to collapse for no apparent reason.

• The dough may have contained a high proportion of cheese or too much fresh onion or garlic.

The crust is shrivelled or wrinkled

Moisture has condensed on the top of the cooked loaf. Remove the bread from the machine as soon as the cycle has finished.

There are deposits of flour on the sides of the loaf

Sometimes dry ingredients stick to the sides of the pan during kneading and then stick unmixed to the risen dough. Check the dough while it is mixing and carefully scrape down the sides of the pan with a plastic spatula to ensure all the flour is incorporated.

The bread has a crumbly, coarse texture

The bread rose too much or the dough was too dry. Either reduce the amount of yeast slightly next time or add more liquid to make a more pliable dough.

The bread has not baked in the centre or on top

There are a number of possibilities:

• The dough was too wet because too much liquid was added. Add less liquid next time and check the dough when mixing, making any necessary adjustments during the kneading cycle.

• The quantities for the recipe were too much for your machine and it could not bake the loaf effectively.

• The dough was too rich. It may have contained too much fat, sugar or egg.

The crust is burnt

There could be too much sugar in the dough. Use less sugar or try the 'light' crust setting next time. The sweet bread setting will also be better for producing a lighter crust.

The loaf is very pale

Choose one of the following solutions:
• Add milk, either dried or fresh, to the dough as this encourages browning.
• Select the dark crust option if your machine has one.
• Increase the sugar content slightly.
• Experiment with different glazes (see page 163).

The crust is too chewy and tough

Increase the fat content of the loaf by adding a little more butter, oil or milk.

Added ingredients were chopped up instead of remaining whole

The ingredients were added at the beginning of the cycle. Add ingredients like fruit and nuts when the machine bleeps or towards the end of the second kneading cycle, according to the instructions in your manufacturer's handbook. Also try leaving fruit and nuts in larger pieces when they are added.

Added ingredients were not mixed in properly

They were added too late in the kneading cycle. Add them a little earlier next time.

The bread is dry

The bread was left uncovered to cool too long and has dried out or the bread has been stored in the fridge. Breads low in fat or made on the French bread cycle dry out very quickly and are best eaten on the day they are baked.

The bread has a holey texture

Either the dough was too wet or the salt was omitted from the dough. Warm weather or high humidity can also cause the dough to rise too quickly.

The bread is difficult to cut and squashes easily when sliced

Either the bread was cut immediately after baking or it was not allowed sufficient time to cool before slicing.

The slices are doughy and tacky

Either the bread was cut immediately after baking or it was not allowed sufficient time to cool before slicing.

Recipe Notes
and Conversion Charts

Flour Conversions

These conversions are for flour only and are based on the 225 ml/8 fl oz plastic cup measure supplied with most bread machines. These conversions WILL NOT be applicable to other dry ingredients as 1 cup of flour will weigh a different amount from, say, 1 cup of walnuts or 1 cup of grated cheese.

25 g	1 oz	
50 g	2 oz	
70 g	2$\frac{1}{2}$ oz	$\frac{1}{2}$ cup
75 g	3 oz	$\frac{5}{8}$ cup
100 g	3 $\frac{1}{2}$ oz	$\frac{3}{4}$ cup
125 g	4 oz	$\frac{7}{8}$ cup
150 g	5 $\frac{1}{4}$ oz	1 cup
175 g	6 oz	
190 g	6$\frac{1}{2}$ oz	1$\frac{1}{4}$ cups
200 g	7 oz	
225 g	8 oz	1$\frac{1}{2}$ cups
250 g	9 oz	1$\frac{3}{4}$ cups
275 g	10 oz	
300 g	11 oz	2 cups
350 g	12 oz	
375 g	13 oz	2$\frac{1}{2}$ cups
400 g	14 oz	2$\frac{3}{4}$ cups
425 g	15oz	
450 g	16 oz/1 lb	3 cups
475 g	17oz	
500 g	17 $\frac{1}{2}$ oz	3$\frac{1}{2}$ cups
525 g	18 $\frac{1}{2}$ oz	
550 g	19 $\frac{1}{2}$ oz	
575 g	20 oz	3$\frac{7}{8}$ cups
600 g	21 oz	4 cups

Liquid Conversions

25 ml	1 fl oz	1/8 cup
50 ml	2 fl oz	1/4 cup
75 ml	3 fl oz	3/8 cup
125 ml	4 fl oz	1/2 cup
150 ml	5 fl oz	5/8 cup
175 ml	6 fl oz	3/4 cup
200 ml	7 fl oz	7/8 cup
225 ml	8 fl oz	1 cup
250 ml	9 fl oz	1 1/8 cups
275 ml	10 fl oz	1 1/4 cups
300 ml	11 fl oz	1 3/8 cups
350 ml	12 fl oz	1 1/2 cups
375 ml	13 fl oz	1 5/8 cups
400 ml	14 fl oz	1 3/4 cups
425 ml	15 fl oz	1 7/8 cups
450 ml	16 fl oz	2 cups

Important Notes

• Measure your ingredients carefully. Take time to allow liquid to settle in the measure on a level surface and read at eye level. For flour, tap the cup lightly to level the surface, but do not squash the flour or other ingredients into the cup.

• Always use the plastic spoon measure supplied with your bread machine for all tsp and tbsp measuring. NEVER use household cutlery as these vary greatly in capacity and can lead to inaccurate measuring of ingredients and poor results.

• If you prefer to use grams and ounces, I would recommend investing in a set of digital scales to measure ingredients for your breadmaking. Most of these scales will measure both wet and dry ingredients.

• Use one set of measures only; never mix metric, imperial or cups in the same recipe.

• Always check that the total amount of flour in a recipe does not exceed the maximum recommended in your manufacturer's handbook. If your machine makes different sizes of loaf, check which setting is applicable for the chosen recipe.

• In the Basic Breads chapter, quantities given in brackets are for larger size loaves.

Stockists and Suppliers

FLOUR, YEAST AND INGREDIENTS

Allinson Baking Club
(flours and yeast)
Tel: 08702 40 2237
www.bakingmad.com

Allergyfree Direct
(speciality flours and
xanthum gum)
Tel: 01865 722003
www.allergyfreedirect.co.uk

Claybrooke Mill
(flours and baking products)
Tel: 01455 202443

DE GUSTIBUS

Tel: 01235 555777
www.degustibus.co.uk

Retail outlets:
4 Southwark Street,
London SE1 1TQ
Tel: 020 7407 3625

53/55 Carter Lane
London EC4 5AE
Tel: 020 7236 0057

53 Blandford Street
London W1H 3AF
Tel: 020 7486 6608

Doves Farm
(speciality flours)
Tel: 01488 684880
www.dovesfarm.co.uk

Sainsbury's
(flours, yeast and xanthum gum)
Tel: 0800 636262
www.sainsbury.co.uk

SPECIAL DIETS AND ALLERGIES

Anaphylaxis Campaign
Tel: 01252 542029
www.anaphylaxis.org.uk

British Allergy Foundation
Tel: 020 8303 8583
www.allergyfoundation.com

British Dietetic Association
Tel: 01212 008080
www.bda.uk.com

British Heart Foundation
Tel: 020 7935 0185
www.bhf.org.uk

Coeliac UK
Tel: 01494 437278
www.coeliac.co.uk

Diabetes UK
Tel: 020 7424 1000
www.diabetes.org.uk

National Asthma Campaign
Tel: 020 7226 2260
www.asthma.org.uk

National Eczema Society
Tel: 020 7281 3553
www.eczema.org.uk

BREAD MACHINE MANUFACTURERS

Electrolux (via Currys)
Tel: 08701 545570
www.currys.co.uk

Morphy Richards
Tel: 08450 777700
www.morphyrichards.com

Panasonic
Tel: 08705 357357
www.panasonic.co.uk

Prima International
Tel: 01132 511500
www.prima-international.com

Pulse Home Products Ltd
(Breville)
Tel: 01616 216900
www.breville.co.uk

Russell Hobbs
Tel: 01619 473000
www.russellhobbs.com

Index

Acknowledgements

Special thanks to:

My husband Simon, for his unwavering encouragement and support and for tasting endless loaves of bread.

Norman Allison for seeing life for this book even after Sonia's sad and sudden death.

Sheila Watson, my agent, and Grace Cheetham from Ebury for their belief and direction in bringing this book to fruition. Not forgetting Amanda Howard for her good-humoured guidance and help with the copy.

My great friend Dan DeGustibus for sharing his knowledge, unique expertise and for supplying encouragement together with his special brand of humour throughout the project.

My avid proofreading team – Gill, Gilly, Teresa and Debs – and all those who over the months have sampled and reported back on hundreds of loaves of bread.

The suppliers who helped me along the way: Allinson for yeast and flour; Doves Farm for speciality flours; and all the breadmaker manufacturers who loaned me machines.